DATE DUE

AP 8 '85			
	45230		Printed in USA

AFFORDABLE HOUSING

AFFORDABLE HOUSING: NEW POLICIES FOR THE HOUSING AND MORTGAGE MARKETS

A Twentieth Century Fund Report by
KENNETH T. ROSEN

BALLINGER PUBLISHING COMPANY
Cambridge, Massachusetts
A Subsidiary of Harper & Row, Publishers, Inc.

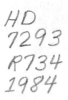

International Standard Book Number: 0-88730-005-7

Library of Congress Catalog Card Number: 84-12419

Printed in the United States of America

Library of Congress Cataloging in Publication Data

Rosen, Kenneth T.

  Affordable housing.

  Includes bibliographical references and index.
  1. Housing policy—United States. 2. Housing—United States—Finance. 3. Mortgages—United States.
I. Twentieth Century Fund. II. Title.
HD7293.R734   1984   363.5′0973   84-12419
ISBN 0-88730-005-7

The Twentieth Century Fund is an independent research foundation which undertakes policy studies of economic, political, and social institutions and issues. The fund was founded in 1919 and endowed by Edward A. Filene.

*

Contents

*

List of Figures

*

List of Tables

*

Foreword

Time was when owning a home of one's own was the American dream. During the first two decades of the postwar period, that dream was realized by an impressive number of Americans. In 1944, while war was still being waged on two fronts, the Fund published a major study entitled *American Housing,* which advocated placing the building of homes at the top of the national policy agenda once peace was won. That study recommended many of the policies that promoted the great postwar boom in home building; it had some unintended consequences as well, such as the vast exodus from the nation's cities to the suburbs.

The policies that so successfully provided good and affordable housing for so long lost their effectiveness with the advent of stagflation in the 1970s. The cost of housing soared along with the interest rates on mortgages. Suddenly, housing came close to being an impossible dream. So the Fund began searching for a scholar to undertake a new study of mortgage and housing policy, one who would take into account changing conditions and analyze what might be done to bring housing into the reach of the new generation of Americans; we wanted a study that would do what our study some forty years ago did.

We found an ideal candidate in Kenneth Rosen, a bright and able economist then at Princeton University's Woodrow Wilson School of Public Policy. Rosen had had a major hand in drafting the Young Families Housing Finance Act, and had a grasp of the intricacies of the mortgage market that few theorists possess. He also was knowledgeable about the multiplicity of agencies and regulations that play a role in stabilizing the market through the mortgage finance system. He was eager to accept the daunting task of taking a fresh and hard look at what ought to be done to make good housing affordable once again.

Now the chairman of the Center for Real Estate and Urban Economics at the University of California at Berkeley, Rosen has examined how the current problems in housing emerged, the measures, mostly faulty, that were fashioned to deal with them, and the policy changes he considers necessary for restoring the wellbeing of the ailing home construction industry. As he sees it, past mistakes in government programs (along with a series of government failures, both of commission and omission) aimed at countering the stagflation of the late 1970s and early 1980s combined with sociological and demographic changes to cripple housing. He recognizes that because housing was looked upon as a social as well as an economic good, it was originally a sheltered industry, and that once it was exposed to all of the elements, it faltered.

Rosen believes that the housing industry can be resuscitated. He suggests that even given the Reagan administration's efforts to encourage market forces, there are ways in which some government assistance for housing makes economic and social sense. He recommends a number of policies that, taken together, should make the dream a reality once more.

The Fund is grateful to Rosen for the job he has done. We think his clear analysis and sensible proposals make a useful contribution to a pressing national problem. We hope his work stimulates debate and action.

M. J. Rossant
Director, Twentieth Century Fund
March 1984

*

Acknowledgments

I incurred many debts in preparing this book. Many people provided intellectual support, and numerous organizations in both government and the private sector supplied essential data.

First, I am greatly indebted to my close colleagues, Dwight Jaffee and Larry Smith, who provided many critical insights into the concepts developed in this book. Second, the Twentieth Century Fund provided financial support for this effort. Without their support and guidance this book would have had a much more narrow audience.

I also owe a large debt to the Center for Real Estate and Urban Economics. The Center, as well as supplying financial support for a portion of this work, provided a stimulating intellectual environment. The staff and associates of the Center were always enthusiastic and friendly, even when they had perhaps become satiated with discussions of housing policy.

Finally, I owe my greatest debt to my predecessors in the housing and research field. Leo Grebler and Sherman Maisel have provided a great inspiration and role model.

Chapter 1

Introduction

The American housing industry of the mid-1980s shows many signals of distress. While record numbers of people are reaching the age when home-ownership seems the most attractive way to meet their needs for shelter, many of these young Americans are also being frustrated in their attempts to purchase homes. Mortgage credit, while available, is very costly relative to inflation. While housing production in 1983 and 1984 has recovered from its low levels early in the decade, it is still not meeting pent-up demographic demand. In many areas of the country both the quantity and quality of rental units are inadequate. The experience of the early 1980s and the continuing affordability problem in housing have jeopardized longstanding national housing goals and a reconsideration of national housing priorities is appropriate and necessary.

The housing crisis of the early 1980s was rooted in unprecedented economic conditions and demographic trends as well as piecemeal, shortsighted policy prescriptions at all levels of government. While the housing and mortgage markets have shown a substantial recovery over the past two years, the problems of the early 1980s are likely to reoccur. In order to avoid repeating past policy failures, policymakers and the public have to be made aware of complex problems facing the housing and housing finance system. This book is designed to provide a useful primer in that educational effort and an intelligible guide for those interested in contributing to the policy formation process for the housing and housing finance industries.

Goals of National Housing Policy

Ensuring adequate shelter — "a decent home in a suitable living environment," in the language of the Housing Act of 1948 — has long been a goal of national housing policy. Homeownership has been encouraged by a combination of mortgage and tax policies, and the supply of low- and middle-income rental housing has been promoted by an array of direct and indirect programs. This dual focus has, until the past several years, reflected the national consensus about the role of housing in society. Homeownership has been an explicit priority in American domestic policy since the end of World War II, when the federal government set up programs to encourage veterans to purchase homes. Federal mortgage subsidy programs, tax incentives, and low-interest, long-term mortgage loans have since enabled two-thirds of all American households and 87 percent of those families in the prime household formation age group (thirty-five to sixty-four) to own homes.

There are sound theoretical arguments for the apparent federal preference for policies promoting ownership over renting in meeting shelter objectives. The sociological and psychological nature of housing consumption distinguishes it from other economic goods. Homeownership provides a feeling of security, a sense of accomplishment from each ounce of sweat equity expended to improve that security, and a means by which individuals can exercise greater control over their destinies.

Housing is also critical in defining the nature and the extent of social interactions. The location of the home helps determine peer groups and influences accessibility to employment and educational opportunities for the household. The location and the quality of the home often serve as measurements of self-worth and social status as well.

Housing also has many "merit good" characteristics. For example, purchase and maintenance expenditure decisions can have tangible and significant effects on the value of surrounding properties. Without government incentives, individuals might inefficiently underinvest in housing. Because of this social aspect of housing, American domestic policy has emphasized meeting housing goals through homeownership.

The success of these policies is indicated by the sharp rise in homeownership and the sharp decline in substandard housing since World War II. Now the central themes of housing policy must be to make housing more affordable to the new generation of young Americans entering the housing market and to ensure a supply of new housing adequate to meet the growing demand of the 1980s. This would prevent periodic housing shortages, with attendant price spirals, and allow continued mobility to meet changing employment patterns.

Because housing plays a central role in the national economy, policy geared to ensure stability in housing production over time may be desirable. The housing delivery system may only be able to provide an adequate supply of affordable homes in a relatively stable environment. It is critical to define carefully the stability desired if one is to avoid inducing rigidity and a lack of responsiveness to changing demand patterns on the part of the housing supply system.

Particularly in an era of competing demands for scarce public resources, the efficient use of housing subsidy funds is essential. Equity goals should not be set aside, however; how a nation shelters less advantaged households is a test of its commitment to economic justice. National housing policies and resources directed at those who are disadvantaged (low- and middle-income households in inadequate housing) is also a social investment that offers a potentially large return in comparison with programs providing the largest subsidies to those who consume luxury *investment* housing. Equity and efficiency goals may well go hand in hand for the housing industry.

Finally, national housing goals and policies must recognize those who do not wish or cannot afford to own a home. The provision of an adequate supply of affordable rental housing may be best achieved by policies aimed at stimulating new construction and rehabilitation of the existing stock of houses.

These goals for emerging national housing policies represent no major shift in social priorities from those underlying the Housing Act of 1948. They may be thought of as first steps in the direction of developing operational goals for policymakers interested in assuming access to "a decent home in a suitable living environment at an affordable cost" for all Americans. However, they are not yet operational, inasmuch as definitions of key terms — "adequate supply" and "affordable cost," for example — are not provided. We attempt to provide such definitions in this book.[1]

Housing Market Conditions in the Early 1980s

The housing market in the early 1980s could be best characterized as being in a state of depression. Housing starts fell off appreciably. Home sales dropped by nearly 50 percent. Even house prices fell by over 10 percent, a remarkable occurrence in a period of relatively high inflation. This represents an even sharper relative decline in "real" housing values than that which occurred during the Great Depression, when house prices fell in concert with all other prices. Housing activity peaked in 1978–79 and then began to plummet steadily. Three bad housing years (1980 through 1982) caused a momentous displacement in the homebuilding and housing finance industries, primarily as a result of federal macropolicy mismanagement.

The response of the Reagan administration to this depression and crisis was very different from that of earlier administrations faced with similar problems. Previously, the distress of housing would encourage the federal government to provide some programs to assist the consumer and the industry in this area. The Reagan administration not only refrained from helping the industry but actually accelerated the process of dismantling the entire set of support programs that have made the housing industry so successful for the past fifty years. Thus, the housing crisis of the early 1980s was created not only by macropolicy error and macroeconomic conditions, but also by the transition crisis created by the removal of the traditional supportive role of the federal government.

Though the magnitude of the crisis in the early 1980s was new, cyclical instability in housing construction is not. The situation from 1980–1982 was unique in that the federal government was not making use of sector-specific policies to aid the housing sector. In the early 1980s federal policy was moving in precisely the opposite direction. No explicit attempt was made even to ease the transition problem; no countercyclical housing programs were put forth in the midst of the worst cyclical decline in the recent history of housing.

Some portion of the responsibility for present housing conditions must be assigned to the overheated conditions of the late 1970s. The sharp rise in house prices certainly led to overinvestment of certain households in housing and attracted speculators. This overinvestment partly had to be self-corrective. With the runaway house prices of the 1970s a thing of the past, the investment motive for housing purchases has been greatly reduced. The downsizing of new American houses can be seen as an adaptation to this, similar in some respects to the downsizing of American cars in response to the crisis in the automotive industry that was primarily a result of the increases in the price of oil. Unless there is strong growth in the economy, or a reversal of the trend toward smaller households, smaller homes will be built on smaller lots to meet the demands for shelter and the financial situations of the vast number of people coming on the market. While there has been a substantial recovery in the economy in 1983 and 1984, it is only a matter of time before we enter another period of crisis like that of the 1980–1982 period.

The Effects of Macroeconomic Policy on Housing

The prime cause of the housing disaster of the early 1980s was the severe economywide recession induced by continued tight Federal Reserve Board (FRB) monetary policy. With unemployment in construction approaching 20 percent, the lumber industry nearly completely shut down, suppliers of materials experiencing large losses, and the housing finance system on the verge of bankruptcy, some change in federal monetary policy clearly was necessary.

The real rate of interest is at its highest level since the Great Depression. The real interest rate is the nominal rate of interest minus the expected rate of inflation. It reflects the actual price paid for money borrowed today and returned tomorrow. The inflation premium in the interest rate merely restores the original purchasing power of the money. During most of the post-World War II period, the real mortgage rate was about 3 percent; in the early 1980s it ballooned to 8 or 9 percent. Even in early 1984 the real mortgage rate remained over 7 percent. In 1980 and 1981 these high real rates were primarily a consequence of a very slow growth in money supply. Since nominal inflation rates actually exceeded nominal money growth rates during these years, a sharp decline in real money supply was the actual result, and the price of money soared in consequence. The recent volatility of monetary policy has induced great uncertainty in financial markets, putting still more upward pressure on real interest rates.

By 1983 and 1984 the real interest rate problem had shifted from a monetary to a fiscal policy cause. Large prospective federal budget deficits are clearly the major problem. Deficits of $200 billion per year for the foreseeable future are providing financial markets with an acute case of indigestion. A 40 to 50 percent increase in the national debt in three years is unacceptable and cannot possibly be funded without a substantial resurgence of inflation or continued high real interest rates. The potential massive deficits are primarily caused by overly aggressive tax cuts and continued runaway growth in the largest portions of the federal budget, namely defense expenditures, transfer payments, and interest payments.

MICROECONOMIC ASPECTS OF THE HOUSING CRISIS

The Demand for Housing Units

One of the most commonly perceived "facts" about the housing market is that the mid-1980s will be a period of spectacularly high levels of housing demand. According to this view, a demographic surge in the 1980s, resulting from the maturation of the post-World War II "baby boom" babies, will lead to an unprecedented demand for housing units in this decade.

The conventional wisdom concerning this enormous demand for housing units in the 1980s is essentially correct. The forecasts developed in Chapter 2 show an effective demand for 21 million additional units. While somewhat lower than the estimates based on conventional wisdom, this still represents an enormous demand for shelter in the 1980s.

The implications of this huge demand are of vital importance. Policymakers on the national level clearly must prepare for it by setting priorities so that housing can compete against alternative goals of increasing national defense spending and reindustrialization. State and local levels of government must also be concerned, for the surge in aggregate demand can affect land-use policies, demand for infrastructure, and basic levels of government services. Business and industry must be prepared for an increased housing demand so that they will be able to meet required higher levels of production. For ordinary citizens the most obvious ramifications of this aggregate demand surge could be even higher relative housing prices.

The Affordability of Housing

There is a long tradition among housing analysts (including this author) of declaring "housing crises" in relation to the affordability of housing. In the 1960s the cost of credit appeared to create major problems. In the 1970s the rising price of houses was the prime villain. In the early 1980s a combination of high prices and record high interest rates led to claims that only 7 percent of families could afford the median-priced home. The collapse of the single-family home market from 1980 to 1982 seemed to provide some evidence confirming these alarmist views.

On the other hand, there were also some positive developments. The vast majority of homeowners made huge capital gains on their housing investment in the 1970s; the majority of renters saw their "real rent," or the change in the rental component of the consumer price index (CPI) minus the change in the overall CPI, decline substantially in the same period. Thus, there is a need for a careful interpretation of the affordability question before a crisis can be declared and policies derived.

Using the conventional measure of affordability (a ratio of current mortgage payments to current income) the early 1980s showed and the mid-1980s will continue to show an affordability crisis for first-time homebuyers. Using an alternative measure—the capital cost of housing, which includes tax benefits and capital gains—provides a somewhat different conclusion. Housing is still affordable if only the household could overcome the initial entry barriers represented by the fixed-payment mortgage and down payment requirements.

The Supply of Mortgage Funds

Although the supply and the demand for housing are the fundamental forces influencing the housing market, the availability and the price of mortgage credit also have a critical influence, particularly on the way supply and demand decisions are made. Translating demand for housing into demand for mortgage credit involves separating demand into three key elements: the demand for new construction financing, the demand for resale financing, and the demand for the refinancing of existing homes without the household moving. The large demand for new construction financing and the pent-up demand for monetization of the large equity position accumulated by households in the late 1970s should lead to an enormous demand for mortgage credit in the 1980s.

This demand for mortgage credit will be juxtaposed against a declining flow of mortgage credit from traditional sources — the savings and loan associations (SLAs). These conflicting pressures of sharply rising demand for mortgage credit and reduced supply from traditional thrift institution lenders in the 1980s can be summarized as creating a growing "mortgage credit gap." This gap will induce major adjustments in the sources and relative price of mortgage credit as market and policy forces adjust to new conditions. The secondary mortgage market will be a critical factor in meeting this demand for mortgage credit.

Cyclical Instability

The periodic cyclical declines in new housing construction lead to widespread shutdowns and curtailment of activities in the construction industry, idle plant and capital equipment in a number of related industries, and sharp rises in the inventory of unsold homes and building-related products.

In addition to the short-run macroeconomic distress that the housing cycle creates, cyclical instability also has long-run consequences for the efficiency of the homebuilding industry. In adapting to instability the industry is forced to use labor-intensive technology, which may be inefficient. This makes it possible to lay off resources — labor — during periods of slow construction activity, thus minimizing costs. While efficient over a wide range of outputs, this may be inefficient at any particular output level. Capital and labor resources are less specialized than in a more stable environment. Start-up and shutdown costs (which involve bankruptcy) may be substantial. Sharp declines in activity increase inventory holding costs throughout the housing production systems.

Public policy toward the cyclical instability in residential construction is based on the premise that cyclical instability in mortgage lending causes fluctuations in housing activity. As a result, since the mid-1960s stabilizing the flow of mortgage credit to the housing market has been a major goal of federal housing policy. The establishment of the Federal Home Loan Mortgage Corporation (FHLMC) and the Federal National Mortgage Association (FNMA), the new aggressiveness of the Federal Home Loan Bank Board (FHLBB), and the reorientation of the Government National Mortgage Association (GNMA) were all at least partial attempts to insulate the mortgage and housing markets from general financial restraint. The activities of these agencies have led to an increased federalization of the private housing finance system.

Land-Use and Rent Control Regulations

Significant government policy responses to the problems of the housing market have also come at the local level, primarily in two areas: land-use regulations and rent control.

Land-use controls enacted for environmental reasons or to regulate growth may be quite effective and desirable, but they are frequently in direct conflict with national and regional housing needs. The constraints imposed on the housing market by these regulations are a direct cause of the housing problem, leading to both shortages and increased housing prices.

Rent control has been initiated on the local level as a response to these shortages and rapidly rising prices in the rental submarket. However, while from the local government perspective rent controls appear to be a reasonable solution, this view is very shortsighted, for in the long run, rent control actually intensifies the rental housing problem by depressing the expected return to investment in rental units and so creates shortages in and under-maintenance of the housing stock.

The Restructuring of the Housing Finance System

Recent government policy actions have initiated a major restructuring of the system that provided mortgage credit for the purchase of owner-occupied housing for the past five decades. The foundations of the old system were regulated deposit interest rates at financial institutions, providing comparative advantages to mortgage lenders; the use of long-term fixed rate and fixed-payment mortgage instruments; and the predominance of thrift institutions — SLAs and mutual savings banks (MSBs) — in mortgage originations and mortgage portfolio holdings. The new mortgage market of the late 1970s and the mid-1980s is marked by "creative financing," "secondary-market transactions," "mortgage passthrough securities," "collateralized mortgage obligations" (CMOs), deregulated deposit markets, tax-exempt "all savers certificates," and an array of adjustable-rate, graduated-payment, and short-term mortgage instruments. The new mortgage mechanisms of the 1980s have arisen primarily as a response to market conditions highlighted earlier.

The Role of the Federal and "Quasi-Federal" Agencies in the Restructured Housing Finance System

The restructuring of the private financial system may greatly alter the traditional roles of the key government and quasi-government agencies dealing with the housing finance system. The eventual complete deregulation of the liability structure of private financial institutions will allow these institutions to compete for deposit funds on the basis of yield to savers. This in turn should reduce the periodic spells of disintermediation from mortgage-lending institutions, whereby depositors withdraw their funds from thrifts to pursue more attractive investment alternatives. Disintermediation has been the main cause of nonprice rationing (i.e., rationing credit by increasing down payment requirements or by not making loans) of mortgage credit and cyclical instability in housing production. It may, however, create a new form of instability caused by interest rate fluctuations, which the agencies may try to moderate.

In addition to combating the likely continued instability in housing production, the agencies will also be called upon to help fill the mortgage credit gap described earlier. The excess demand for mortgage credit and the Reagan administration's desire to reduce the guarantor role of the Federal Housing Administration (FHA) and GNMA will require the remaining agencies to devise an innovative set of nongovernment programs to facilitate the required supply of mortgage credit in the mid-1980s.

REEXAMINING U.S. HOUSING POLICY: CHANGES IN THE ROLE OF THE FEDERAL GOVERNMENT

The latest housing policy initiatives and retrenchments of the federal government and the policy outlines provided by the President's Commission on Housing will form the foundation of future federal housing policy. The commission was appointed by President Reagan in June 1981 to show his commitment to housing and to seek remedies for the problems that the housing industry and housing consumer were facing. To the latter end, the commission reexamined government policy toward homeownership, federal tax policy and credit programs, rental housing, the use of tax-exempt mortgage bonds, and various public subsidy programs.

Even a casual reading of the commission's report shows that a substantial shift in national housing policies is in the making. In its findings the commission went so far as to suggest that it does no good for the government to try to set goals for housing policy and that no real purpose is served by the effort. Of course, if no goals are set, it is quite difficult to measure the success or failure of policy initiatives.

The commission did, however, have a statement of principles which very much reflected the free market philosophy of the Reagan administration and its feeling that government intervention in markets should be minimal. These principles emphasized reliance on the private sector and the phasing out of government programs on a federalized basis, by the transfer of administrative responsibilities to state and local governments.

These recommendations seem to rely on a number of questionable assumptions. For example, the commission claimed that previous housing credit and production programs have been ineffective. In its opinion, it would be better to rely on the private sector and facilitate housing's access to private sector capital in order to stimulate production of housing. It feels the free market can provide housing at lower prices and make housing more widely available. The commission specifically eschews any attempt to make a definite numerical forecast of future housing need.

A major criticism of the Reagan Commission on Housing is that it appears to start with the bias that government programs should be minimal and that past programs have not been effective and efficient in providing for housing production and credit. Analysts who do not accept this respond that a persuasive case can be made that the set of incentives established for housing and homeownership in the past five decades has been extraordinarily effective at not only producing more housing but also mitigating some of the cyclical impact of macroeconomic policy on housing.

On the other hand, there is certainly a case to be made—and the commission makes it—that Section 8, the large rental construction subsidy program, was a very costly and ineffective use of scarce government resources and was inefficient in providing new rental housing. Also, no one can argue with the commission's recommendations to maximize the use of private resources before calling on federal funds.

The commission provides several broad policy options. It urges a movement away from producer-oriented housing subsidies and toward consumer-oriented housing assistance programs. In principle, this is a reasonable approach for the subsidy programs, especially given the problems with the Section 8 new production program. While the concept of housing assistance grants or housing opportunity grants is good, given the budget cuts and reorientation of the present administration, this is a sham recommendation. A key feature of the consumer housing assistance grants is that they should be envisioned as entitlements to all eligible households. However, there will be no substantial financial resources devoted to this program in the near future. Accordingly, while the concept is fine in theory, in reality it is being used as a tool to phase out production subsidy programs without providing workable replacements.

The commission is also recommending the introduction of a rehabilitation tax credit for residential real estate comparable with that on nonresidential real estate. This would permit a tax credit for rehabilitation expenditures of 15 percent for structures thirty to forty years old and 20 percent for older structures. The purpose of this proposal is to provide parity between residential and commercial rehabilitation. It is an essential ingredient in housing policy if the conversion of nonresidential to residential housing and the upgrading of older stock are to play significant roles in the provision of adequate housing supply.

The commission is also considering the use of some sort of tax incentive to encourage savings for down payments by first-time homebuyers. One version of this proposal originated with the author in the late 1970s and will be discussed in more detail in the concluding policy recommendations. The commission's report highlights the problem first-time homebuyers are having accumulating the "grubstake" to buy their first house, an aspect of the affordability problem discussed in more detail below. Proposals for the housing finance system are intended to stimulate the flow of funds to mortgage lenders and reduce mortgage instrument problems.

The commission has appropriately directed its attention to the need to eliminate barriers to pension fund investment in mortgages, because pension funds provide a very important potential pool of funds for the growth of the secondary mortgage market. In a similar vein, it seeks to broaden asset, liability, and service powers of thrift institutions to allow them to do more than just be specialized mortgage lenders and to compete more effectively in a number of different areas. The presumption is that reducing specialization of thrifts will enable them to strengthen their position in the overall market and to compete more successfully for funds. Without the specialized mortgage lender requirements they will be able and willing to provide a more adequate and stable source of mortgage funds.

The commission correctly recognizes that there must be some other incentives (presumably tax incentives) to encourage other lenders to make up for the diminished mortgage funds supplied by thrifts and also to meet the strong demand for mortgage credit expected in the 1980s.

The commission also strongly endorsed alternative mortgage instruments and the development of an active secondary market by the private sector. Here the commission does not address an essential issue: the federal government has to take a leadership role in providing education and experimentation with new mortgages; it also has to narrow down the types of mortgages that are available to reduce confusion.

Finally, the commission appears to be endorsing administration policies to reduce the federal role in underwriting credit risks in the secondary mortgage market. This basically entails scaling down the GNMA and FHA but may in the future involve attacks on the FNMA and FHLMC. An increased level of private sector participation in secondary markets has been encouraged by several recent deregulation efforts. The recent attempt by the administration to exclude GNMA, FNMA, and FHLMC securities as collateral for CMOs shows its clear intentions to reduce the role of these agencies.

In essence, it is easy to agree with the thrust of the commission housing finance recommendations. The implementation of the commission's recommendations, particularly some sort of mortgage investment tax credit, and possibly refundable tax credit to encourage participation by pension funds, is especially critical. However, these recommendations are likely to founder upon the administration's tight domestic budget policy and corresponding reduction in federal policy options for housing.

The recommendations of the commission about reducing the federal role and yet having the federal government provide incentives is somewhat in conflict. The key proposals of the commission — the housing assistance program and the mortgage tax credit — would involve substantial federal outlays. The commission, because of ideological considerations, fails to state specifically that, whether the federal government provides direct expenditure programs or indirect transfers through federal tax incentives, it has a strong role to play in providing a subsidized or continued adequate below-market supply of credit to accommodate at least the shelter portion of housing demand. The failure to state the case for housing's share of public funds and private resources in a forthright manner, hiding instead behind the rhetoric of free market principles, is perhaps the commission's greatest failing.

NOTE

1. We have carefully avoided extensively addressing the problems of low-income households. The major focus here has been on the moderate-income households and homeownership opportunities for moderate- and middle-income households. We have not attempted to deal with the problem of subsidizing low-income households for homeownership or rental housing. In general, the housing problem of these individuals is low income, a problem that is not amenable to easy solution within the framework of the housing market, but that may require explicit income redistribution policies. The real problem is how to come up with an income maintenance program that would provide proper work incentives for individuals as well as a minimum level of support for all Americans. Housing vouchers similar to food stamps may be a reasonable temporary solution to this problem.

Chapter 2

The Magnitude and Distribution of Housing Demand in the 1980s

Most housing analysts agree that as the baby boom generation matures the demand for housing units in the 1980s will rise to unprecedented levels. Actual estimates vary widely, but the conventional wisdom, which antici-pates this large increase, is essentially correct. Industry and government will have to augment their capacity to provide key materials, labor, public ser-vice support, and appropriate credit financing to meet this increased demand for housing, but they must put their policies in place now to meet the needs of the next three to five years. In order to calculate future growth, accurate information is essential. Yet, while numerous estimates of housing "need" have received extensive publicity, most are deficient in that they fail to account adequately for the impact of changing socioeconomic condi-tions.[1]

Housing demand is usually seen to arise from three sources. The demo-graphic component is produced by population growth and changes in household formation rates; the replacement component arises from depre-ciation, accidental losses, and an upgrading of the housing stock; and the miscellaneous component is composed of additional vacancies to meet the mobility needs of households and the seasonal and secondary-home mar-kets. The projected "need" (or what is erroneously called demand) repre-sented by each component is usually calculated by extrapolating past trends. Since this implicitly assumes that important relationships and trends of the past will not change during the forecast period, the figures derived from such techniques could be misleading given the volatile state of the economy and the significant sociological changes that have occurred and continue today. Basic trends can be altered or even reversed by changes in public policy or economic and sociological conditions. Housing demand for the 1980s will be determined by conditions that can be quite different from those that produced previous statistical trends. Consequently, there is a substantial element of uncertainty that must be taken into account when forecasting housing demand.

It is therefore necessary to reevaluate housing forecast methodologies to predict requirements for the 1980s accurately. Policymakers must have reliable forecasts so that they can correctly plan for the resulting credit demand, infrastructure requirements, and changes and additions to local services. Such forecasts must go beyond merely projecting the total amount of housing required to provide indications of how these incremental units will be distributed between rental and owner-occupied markets and across different geographic regions of the country.

PROJECTING TOTAL HOUSING DEMAND

Housing Demand Induced by Demographic Change

Population and Age Distribution of Population. The size, age distribution, and growth rate by age group of the population are among the most critical factors influencing the nature and extent of shelter requirements. They are also among the most predictable. For a ten-year projection only a segment of the total population is actually relevant. Specifically, the focus of attention is that part of the population now part of the home purchase or rental market or that part which will enter these markets as a separate household unit in the next decade — basically, the population presently over age ten.

In contrast, economic demographers focus on the fertility component of population change, or the expected future growth in population due to birthrate fluctuations. This is less relevant to housing analysts, since the population that will make housing decisions in the next decade is already born. Current birthrate changes will only alter the housing picture in the 1980s through the influence of changes in family size on the size and location of units. These effects are expected to be small and are not included in this analysis.

Only two other factors could appreciably alter the size of the population in terms of housing demand over the next decade: a dramatic variation in the death rate or a major change in net international immigration. The national death rate has been declining moderately for the past several decades and should continue to do so in the near future. Barring any major policy shifts, immigration should also continue to be predictable.

Accordingly, housing analysts are able to construct fairly accurately an age profile of the housing-relevant population for the next decade. Such a profile shows that startling though highly predictable changes in age distribution occurred in the 1970s and are anticipated for the rest of the 1980s. This shifting age distribution was directly caused by changes in the number of births two and three decades ago.

The influence of the baby boom on the age distribution of the population can be examined in two ways. The conventional way of analyzing the changing age distribution of the population is to look at the number and the net change in people in each class. A less common approach emphasizes gross flows in the population age distribution. These alternative perspectives produce somewhat different implications for planners.

The conventional mode of analysis is illustrated in Table 2–1, which indicates that the housing-relevant population is growing older and larger. The population aged fifteen to twenty-four will show an unprecedented decline of slightly over 7 million people by 1990, more than offsetting its growth in the 1970s. This reflects the drop in births that occurred after 1962.

Table 2–1. Population Age Distribution (thousands).

Age Group	Year (actual)			Year (projected)	
	1970	1975	1980	1985	1990
15–24	35,806	40,608 (4,802)	42,470 (1,862) (6,664)	39,543 (−2,927)	35,380 (−4,163) (−7,090)
25–34	25,099	31,246 (6,147)	37,412 (6,166) (12,313)	41,208 (3,796)	42,933 (1,725) (5,521)
35–64	65,047	66,595 (1,548)	70,331 (3,736) (5,284)	76,706 (6,375)	84,366 (7,660) (14,035)
Over 64	20,106	22,620 (2,514)	25,709 (3,089) (5,603)	28,338 (2,629)	31,464 (3,126) (5,755)
Over 14	146,058	161,069 (15,011)	175,992 (14,853) (29,864)	185,795 (9,873)	194,143 (8,348) (18,221)
Over 24	110,252	120,461 (10,209)	133,452 (12,991) (23,200)	146,252 (12,800)	158,763 (12,511) (25,311)

Source: U.S. Bureau of the Census, Population Division.

The ramifications of this decline will be felt most by institutions specializing in providing goods and services to this age group, particularly colleges and universities. The sharp decline in elementary- and high-school enrollments in the 1970s will be reflected in a drastic slump in university and college enrollment in the late 1980s. The impact on the housing market will also be substantial: the decrease in population in this age group should lead to a sharp decline by the end of the decade in the demand for rental housing and mobile homes, as these types of housing units are traditionally occupied by younger households.

The growth rate in the population aged twenty-five to thirty-four also slows in the 1980s. This group, which grew by nearly 11 million people in the 1970s, will add only 5 million individuals in the 1980s. Nearly 70 percent of this increase will be realized by the middle of the decade. Since this group has historically provided most first-time homebuyers, the abatement of growth in the 1980s will have significant effects on the extent and nature of new construction, especially after 1985.

In the 1980s, however, the effect of the baby boom bulge shows up most dramatically in the age group of those thirty-five to sixty-four years old. This group increased by about 5.3 million people in the 1970s and will add almost three times that number in the 1980s. While it remains an important source of the stock demand for housing, many of the members of this group are in households that own rather than rent housing units prior to entering this age category. Younger members of this group—those aged thirty-five to forty-four—may still be switching from renter to owner status, but their contribution to incremental housing unit demand is relatively small.

The population over sixty-five shows remarkably stable growth. They added nearly 5 million people in the 1970s and will add about the same number by 1990. The proportion of people in this class of the housing-relevant population also rises throughout the 1980s.

Aggregating age categories to obtain an overall population change profile uncovers some interesting trends. The growth in population aged fifteen or more declines steadily over these two decades: over 29 million people entered this group over the period, but only 18 million more are expected by 1990. The five-year comparisons vividly demonstrate the secular decline in growth of the adult population to be housed in rental or owner-occupied units. If the population aged fifteen to twenty-four is excluded from these aggregate figures, however, numerical growth of the adult population stabilizes considerably. Increments to the prime homeownership population in the range of 2 to 3 million persons per year are indicated for the 1980s.

It is clear that this measure of demographic change (net population movement by age class) does not entirely support the bullish projections of housing analysts, as net population growth numbers in the first-time home purchase and apartment rental groups slow down dramatically in the 1980s.

In contrast, a gross flow measure of the age distribution of the population shows a somewhat larger and later peak in the groups most likely to purchase homes. Simple scrutiny of historical birth statistics is sufficient for this analysis. (See Figure 2-1.) The number of births peaked over the period 1957-1961. Not surprisingly, then, the number of people entering the prime first-time home purchase bracket (twenty-five to thirty-four) will peak during the 1982-1987 period. By definition, this also means that record numbers of people will be departing from prime rental and mobile home markets. On average, some 4.2 million people will make this transition annually. Thus, in a gross inflow sense, with many first-time home demanders coming into the market, the housing market looks strong in the 1980s. It is our view that the gross demand for housing most accurately reflects the potential demand for housing in the 1980s.

The Household Formation Process.   Whether a net or gross flow measure is employed, it is apparent that substantial additional housing units are needed for the 1980s. But a direct translation of these changes into additional housing demand would be a mistake, for a wide range of uncertainty results from the forces that influence household formation rates. Housing requirements do not depend on the age distribution of the population alone, but also on the interaction of age distribution with the ways in which people decide to group themselves into household units. These decisions are sensitive to an array of economic and social forces.

A household is defined as a group of people occupying a housing unit. Two major categories of households are commonly identified, and they are distinguished by the relationship between household members and the household head. (By definition, a household has only one head.) A family household exists when all occupants are related to the household head by blood, marriage, or adoption. A primary individual household, on the other hand, refers either to a person living alone or to one living with nonrelatives.

The number and type of households consequently depend not only on the age structure of the population but also on the way in which the population establishes or breaks family ties and groups itself into shelter-consuming units. In the past decade large numbers of people who previously would have been family household heads or members have chosen to form individual households. In 1970 some four-fifths of the 63.8 million households in the United States were classified as families. By 1980 another 17.4 million households had been formed, yet more than half of these were of the primary individual type. The number of individual households almost doubled in this period.

Table 2-2 indicates that the trend toward individual households is especially concentrated among young households. Household headship rates (the ratio of the number of household heads in an age group to the size of

Figure 2–1. Annual Live Births.

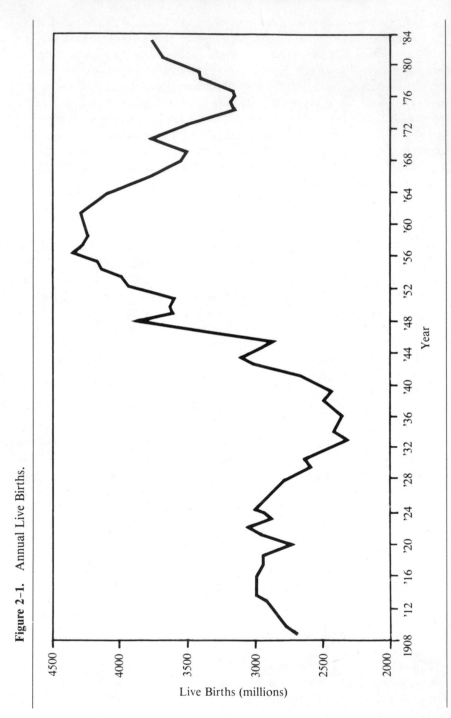

Table 2-2. Age-Specific Household Headship Rates, 1960-1980.

	Primary Individuals				Primary Families			
Year	24 or Less	25–34	35–44	65 and Over	24 or Less	25–34	35–64	65 and Over
1960	.013	.026	.062	.196	.094	.402	.456	.371
1965	.017	.031	.067	.229	.097	.417	.459	.368
1970	.025	.045	.073	.262	.099	.426	.467	.356
1975	.041	.076	.083	.278	.104	.415	.465	.366
1980	.065	.116	.095	.295	.090	.383	.464	.312

Source: U.S. Bureau of the Census, Population Division.

that group) for the primary individual households have been rising for all age groups over the past two decades. Delayed marriage, living with a person of the opposite sex, the uncoupling of existing households by divorce, and the preference and ability of surviving elderly spouses to retain their own living quarters have all led to the increase in primary individual households. These dramatic socioeconomic changes affecting all age groups have led to a substantial increase in the demand for housing units.

There has been a fourfold increase in the proportion of the population under age thirty-five heading separate households. In terms of actual numbers of households, this effect is even more dramatic because these are the baby boom age groups. The increase in the proportion of people over age thirty-five in primary individual households is somewhat less dramatic but still highly significant.

In contrast, while the individual headship rate has soared, the family headship rate has remained largely unchanged in the same period. These two trends have resulted in a dramatic increase in the "household yield," or the number of households forming from the population as a whole.

A reduction in family household size and a drop in the proportion, but not the number, of households classified as families have accompanied these trends. The young individuals who move out of their parents' homes increase the individual household headship rate without decreasing the family headship rate. A divorce in which children are present has the same effect, for the spouse with custody of the children has remained a family household, while the other spouse has become a primary individual household. These are not arbitrary distinctions; they represent an increase in the real demand for separate housing units.

Table 2-3 provides further evidence of this fundamental restructuring of American living habits. These distributions confirm that there has been a massive shift toward nontraditional types of households, as suggested by

Table 2-3. Households by Types.

	Year			Percentage Change	
	1980	*1970*	*1960*	*1970 to 1980*	*1960 to 1970*
Total households	80,776	63,401	52,799	27.4	20.1
Percentage of total					
Family	73.7	81.2	85.0	15.7	14.6
Husband–wife	60.8	70.5	74.3	9.8	13.9
Male head (no wife)	2.1	1.9	2.3	41.4	–
Female head (no husband)	10.8	8.7	8.4	58.3	24.4
Nonfamily	26.3	18.8	15.0	77.7	51.3
Living alone	22.7	17.1	13.1	68.6	57.4
Living with person	3.6	1.7	1.9	167.8	9.5
Unmarried couples with no children	1.4	0.5	–	247.0	–

Source: U.S. Bureau of the Census, Population Division.

Table 2-2. Traditional husband and wife family units have grown more slowly than any other type of household, showing a 9.8 percent increase from 1970 to 1980. On the other hand, nonfamily households showed an increase of over 70 percent during the same time period, divorced female households increased 135 percent, single female households increased 118 percent, and persons of opposite sex sharing the same living quarters rose an astounding 247 percent. In terms of absolute growth, nonfamily and single-parent-headed households accounted for 9.3 million out of the 17.4 million households formed in the 1970–80 period.

Forecasting Household Headship Rates

Since the age distribution of the population is well determined for the next ten years, the major source of uncertainty in estimating total housing demand is the path of household headship rates. A switch toward individual households greatly increases the household yield for each population group and thus increases the demand for housing. If accurate forecasts of age-specific headship rates for different household types were available, the problem of projecting housing requirements would be trivial, entailing only simple arithmetic operations. Previous research has isolated three key factors that help determine secular trends in age-specific headship rates.[2]

The first and most obvious factor is the level of real income per household, which provides the economic resources for the family or individual to maintain a housing unit. While there has been a rise in real income in the past decade, there has also been a substantial redistribution of income among household types. During the 1970s an increased number of women entered the labor force, out of both choice and necessity. This sharp rise in the female labor participation rate has facilitated the formation of female-headed households. In addition, there was a substantial real increase in social security and other retirement benefits during the same period, enabling the elderly to maintain individual household units. Recent high unemployment rates, slow real income growth, and uncertainty about the future of the social security system suggest that these trends may be moderated in the present decade.

The second key determinant of household formation rates is the cost of operating a housing unit. The surge in households over the past decade was spurred by a drop in the real price of rental housing of nearly 32 percent. Although this may seem implausible, it is a fact that the cost of rental housing increased only two-thirds as much as the cost of all goods and services that enter into calculation of the consumer price index (CPI). An oversupply of rental housing early in the decade, the reluctance of small landlords to raise rents, the prevalence of old fixed-rate financing, and rent control policies in some jurisdictions played a role, but it is difficult to measure just how significant each of these effects was. Since the rental unit is the main type of unit occupied by primary individual households, the causal relationship seems clear: declining real rental cost has encouraged the formation of primary individual households.

In contrast, the cost of homeownership has slightly exceeded the overall inflation rate during this period.[3] Since the relevant housing choice for most family households is homeownership, the relatively constant family household headship rates shown in Table 2-2 are consistent with this price data.

These two economic factors are complemented by a third fundamental determinant of household formation: a strong sociological trend toward individual fulfillment. Individuals born during the postwar baby boom have adopted lifestyles markedly different from those of previous generations. Social experimentation in living arrangements is condoned, if not encouraged. Young people are postponing marriage to pursue higher education and career goals. These proclivities first received formal attention when the Census Bureau added two new categories to its survey: POSSLQ (persons of opposite sex sharing the same living quarters) and PSSSLQ (persons of the same sex sharing the same living quarters). All these factors work in the direction of increasing primary individual headship rates and the need for additional housing.

The desire for individual fulfillment is also reflected in divorce rates, which have doubled since 1965 and have been a major cause of the increase in individual household formations in the age group of those twenty-five to sixty-four years old. This dramatic surge in divorce rates has fundamentally altered the nature of the housing consumer. Besides increasing the number of individual households, this high divorce rate has produced a household with a distinctive history of housing demand. Many divorced households have previously owned their own home and experienced the investment and tax advantages of homeownership. As a result, a divorce is likely to produce a situation in which one spouse attempts to keep the house while the other spouse attempts to regain ownership advantages by purchasing another unit.

The fundamental relationship between marital instability and housing demand can be expanded to include more speculative hypotheses. The rise in female labor force participation can partly be attributed to the increased need of single, married, and divorced females to support or help support the housing unit. A job is a necessary condition to set up a household, unless one is receiving adequate investment income, welfare, or social security benefits. In the case of the traditional family household, the two-earner household may be essential for accumulating the down payment and qualifying for mortgage loans.

Table 2–4 illustrates historical trends in these key economic and sociological factors influencing household formation patterns. Despite a decline in the average size of households over this period, real disposable income per household has been on the rise; rental costs have failed to keep pace with the overall inflation rate, the divorce rate has more than doubled, and female labor participation rates have risen steadily. Since these are the principal determinants of household headship rates, knowledge of the ways in which these factors interact and the values they will take on for the upcoming decade would greatly facilitate projecting housing requirements. This concept of headship rates as functions of economic and sociological factors can be formalized in an econometric model of the household formation process.[4]

This methodology is somewhat more sophisticated than that employed by the Census Bureau in forecasting household formations. Five illustrative forecasts are normally provided by the bureau. All focus directly on observed household headship rates of the past; they differ only in the weight that is given to particular observed values. Some forecasts weight recent observations more heavily than earlier observations in the sample period; others weight all observations equally. Since no compelling reason is offered

Table 2–4. Economic and Sociological Factors Influencing Household Headship Rates.

Year	Real Disposable Income per Person 1972 ($)	Real Disposable Income per Household 1972 ($)	Divorced Family Households	Rent Overall CPI	Home-ownership Overall CPI	Female Labor Participation Rate
1960	2,721	9,242	.009	1.03	0.97	37.8
1965	3,184	10,685	.010	1.03	0.98	39.3
1970	3,684	11,782	.014	0.95	1.11	43.4
1975	4,061	12,102	.018	0.85	1.13	46.4
1980	4,481	12,546	.020	0.78	1.27	50.0

Source: U.S. Bureau of Labor Statistics and U.S. Bureau of the Census.

for choosing one weighting scheme or sample period over another, Census Bureau projections will be used here simply to bracket estimates obtained from our econometric model. Census Bureau estimates of total households in 1990 range from 90 to 99 million, some 9 to 19 million more than existed in 1980. The lower bound is based on an assumption that headship rates for the 1980s will remain the same as they were in 1978. The upper bound is derived from a methodology that gives more weight to recent changes, all of which were increases in headship rates.

In contrast, aggregate household estimates produced by the econometric model for three different economic scenarios (corresponding to low, intermediate, and high growth) range from 95.4 million to 97.4 million households. (See Table 2-5.)

The econometric technique provides a way of quantifying the impact of economic conditions in the forecast period that might differ from those in the historical period. In the 1980s the growth in income and divorce rates are expected to be lower and real rents higher than in the 1970s. Slower growth in income will result from the efforts of economic policymakers to cope with high inflation and energy prices of the past decade. The growth in divorce rates will be lower because many households will have already taken advantage of the freer sociological environment that encouraged more divorces;

Table 2-5. Household Formations.

Total households 1980	81,145
Total households 1990[a]	
1. High economic growth	
Real disposable income increasing 3 percent per year	
Rental component of CPI — overall CPI increasing 1 percent per year	97,387
Change 1980 to 1990	16,242
2. Base economic growth	
Real disposable income increasing 1 percent per year	
Rental component of CPI — overall CPI no change	96,294
Change 1980 to 1990	15,149
3. Low economic growth	
Real disposable income decreasing 0.25 percent per year	
Rental component of CPI — overall CPI decreasing 0.9 percent per year	95,398
Change 1980 to 1990	14,253

[a] Projections by author.

moreover, the general aging of the population will lead to lower divorce rates. Rising rental rates relative to the price of other goods will be induced by a shortage of rental housing in many metropolitan areas. These changes should reduce the rate of growth of household headships relative to the trend in the 1970s. Evidence of this slower trend in household formation was apparent during the serious recession of 1980–82, with net household formations averaging under 1 million per year during this period.

The econometric forecasts of household formations fall in a narrower range than the census forecasts. They also clearly show the sensitivity of household formation to economic conditions. The high and low economic forecasts show a difference of nearly 2 million household formations over the decade, from 14.2 million in the low-growth to 16.2 million in the high-growth forecasts.

Econometric projections and census trend extrapolations show annual household growth that can be translated directly into a demand for housing units in the 1.4 to 1.6 million range in the 1980s. The growth in population and the changing age distribution of the population account for 1.2 million additional households annually. This is the portion of housing demand that is fairly certain. The remaining 0.2 to 0.4 million annual growth in households is a result of household headship rate increases produced by changing economic conditions and sociological trends. Even in the pessimistic case, the demographic changes described above have important implications for housing in the 1980s.

Replacement Housing Demand

The removal of housing units from the existing stock produces an additional housing requirement beyond the incremental need resulting from demographic change. This component of housing demand is difficult to measure because adequate data on changes in the quality and quantity of the housing stock are generally not available.

The major source of replacement demand arises from stock depletion caused by demolitions, fires, floods, and windstorms. In addition, conversion of residential units to nonresidential units and the merging of residential units can also increase the net loss of housing stock. On the other hand, the conversion of nonresidential units to residential units, the subdividing of existing residential units, and the rehabilitation of condemned units can decrease the replacement demand for housing by increasing and preserving the housing stock.

While these types of conversion and alteration activities have been a major source of housing supply during certain periods, they are extremely difficult to document. The best source of housing stock data, the *Annual*

Table 2-6. Changes in Housing Stock, 1970–1980.

	1970[a]	1973	1974	1975	1976	1977	1978	1979	1980
All housing units	70,184	75,969	77,601	79,087	80,881	82,420	84,618	86,374	88,207
Change in stock	—	5,785	1,632	1,468	1,794	1,539	2,198	1,756	1,833
Units completed[b]	—	8,299	2,227	1,653	1,584	1,858	2,148	2,151	1,736
Implicit net removals	—	2,464	595	195	(210)[c]	319	(50)	115	(331)
Implicit removal rate (%)	—	3.24	0.77	0.25	(0.26)	0.39	(0.006)	(0.13)	(0.38)

[a] Adjusted for 1970 census undercount.
[b] Includes mobile homes and public housing.
[c] ( ) implies net addition to the stock.
Source: *Annual Housing Survey* and Decennial Census.

Housing Survey (AHS), does make an attempt to separate permanent and retrievable losses to the housing stock. Permanent losses are units that result from demolition or natural disaster and can never return to the housing inventory. Retrievable losses, on the other hand, move in and out of the stock as a result of conversions, subdivisions, and rehabilitations. Some rough estimates of replacement demand for housing in the 1970s can be obtained from the AHS reports.

An implicit annual net removal rate can be calculated by comparing stock changes with the number of units added. These calculations (see Table 2–6) show a declining trend in net removal rates since the early 1970s. They also show a great deal of volatility, moving from 1.08 percent per year in net removals to a net appreciation rate of 0.26 percent per year. This volatility clearly reflects economic and housing market conditions that critically influence the year-to-year replacement rate. In a recession the replacement rate falls as existing stock is utilized more intensively to offset the shortfall in new production. When new housing production is high, on the other hand, an increased amount of lower quality housing is removed from the stock in response to the looser market conditions.

A final source of demolitions involves the removal of units in order to allow the construction of new housing. During the periods when there are high levels of new construction (especially multifamily construction) a greater number of older units are demolished to make room for this activity. In contrast, during periods of low levels of new construction this source of removals declines substantially.

The second major source of replacement housing demand is conversion and alteration activity. This source involves the two-way movement of units between residential and nonresidential uses and the splitting up or consolidation of residential units. It also includes that portion of the stock temporarily not habitable due to condemnation, vandalism, or disaster, but which can be retrieved for housing use by additional investment. Net additions or losses from conversions and alterations are determined by public policy variables and overall market conditions. Presently, public policy in a number of metropolitan areas has encouraged the conversion of nonresidential structures to residential uses. Similarly, market response to high levels of aggregate demand and to the high price of suburban housing relative to older central-city housing has also made conversion and extensive rehabilitation attractive. By the late 1970s there were actually net additions to the housing stock from these sources.

In summary, the replacement demand for housing is expected to continue its downward trend in the 1980s: very low net removal rates of the mid- and late 1970s will be the norm. The only offsetting factor is the expected high levels of new production in the 1980s, which would encourage site assembly removals.

An average net removal rate of 0.4 percent over the decade, which translates into about 350,000 units per year, is assumed for this analysis. Traditional estimates of the net annual removal rate have ranged from 0.7 percent to 0.9 percent, or 600,000 to 800,000 units per year. These differences
are extremely large and add to the uncertainty of housing demand in the
1980s.

Vacancy and Second-Home Demand

Vacant housing benefits both owners and potential occupants. Vacancies are
desirable to consumers who wish to move within and between metropolitan
areas. They are also desirable to sellers and landlords because housing units
face a market price distribution rather than a single market price. Thus,
there is an "optimal" vacancy rate, which allows sellers and buyers to
sample the market in a search process.

Three basic factors influence the optimal level of vacant units: the mobility rate of the population, the expected variance of the price distribution,
and the holding cost of vacant units. Higher mobility rates increase the
optimal levels of vacant housing units. Greater vacancy rates and mobility
allow landlords to raise rents more frequently by increasing the possibility
of finding new tenants willing to pay higher rents. In addition, the ease of
moving into a vacant unit rather than one that is occupied until a certain
date tends to enhance the desirability of the vacant unit and increase the
value a potential renter places on it.

In the past two decades there has been a general trend toward decreasing
vacancy rates in the rental sector while owner vacancies have been reasonably stable. (See Figure 2–2.) During this period mobility rates were fairly
constant, but interest rates rose dramatically. In the late 1970s the expected
gain from holding vacant rental units declined because of the spread of rent
control. As a result, the optimal vacancy rate has probably declined substantially in the rental sector. Similar forces will be at work in the 1980s;
interest rates should remain high, rent control will remain important in
many areas, and, in contrast to the 1970s, the mobility rate is likely to
decline because of an aging population and decreased employment opportunities. Thus, the optimal rental vacancy rate will decline somewhat further. This suggests little or no incremental demand for vacant rental units
over the decade.

The final element of interest in projecting total housing requirements is
the demand for second homes, primarily vacation units. Despite high expectations because of increased leisure time and incomes, there is little evidence
from the available data that this market is booming. The AHS indicates that
265,000 seasonal units were built between 1970 and 1980, slightly more than

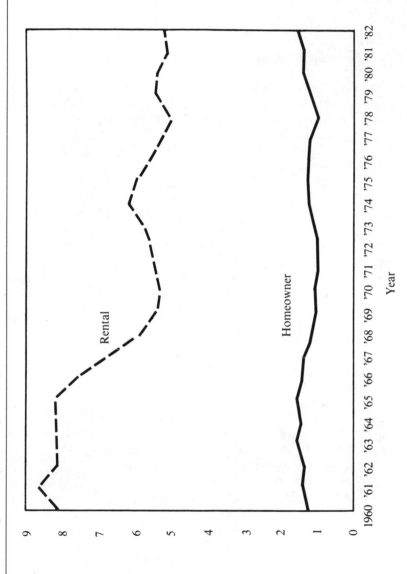

Figure 2-2. Housing Vacancy Rates.

25,000 per year. During the same period a similar number of seasonal units were removed from the stock. Whatever direction this market takes, its impact on incremental housing needs will be small relative to that caused by demographic changes and replacement needs.

Summary of Total Housing Demand for the 1980s

The changing age distribution and the overall growth of the population will, assuming constant headship rates and household sizes, produce a demand for 12 million housing units. Depending on economic conditions, increases in household headship rates can be expected to produce an additional demand for 2 to 4 million housing units. The range of estimates of replacement demand is also wide; a low estimate of removal rates (0.2 percent per year) indicates 1.8 million units over the decade. A most likely estimate (0.4 percent) indicates 3.6 million units over the decade; a high estimate (0.9 percent) would show a demand for 8 million housing units in the 1980s. The other components of demand will contribute at most 350,000 to 400,000 units over the decade.

The demand for housing units in the 1980s will range from nearly 16 million to over 26 million units. The most likely estimates based on our forecasts of economic conditions show an effective demand for 19 million units. This is somewhat lower than conventional wisdom estimates but still represents an enormous demand for shelter in the 1980s.

RENTAL AND HOMEOWNERSHIP MARKETS: THE TENURE CHOICE DECISION

Whether to own or rent a housing unit is a fundamental individual decision that is sensitive to public policy decisions and of great importance to housing analysts. The propensity for homeownership follows a life cycle pattern for both family and individual households.

Young households tend to have higher mobility rates, less secure job prospects, lower incomes, and a smaller amount of wealth; in consequence, they tend to rent housing units. As household heads reach the age of thirty, geographic mobility declines, job prospects and family relationships stabilize, real income rises, and wealth is accumulated. As a result, by the age of thirty-five the vast majority of family households and a substantial minority of individual household heads have chosen to own their own housing unit. Table 2-7 shows a steady rise in ownership as households age, in keeping with the life cycle hypothesis. The figures also demonstrate an across-the-board surge in homeownership for all age groups in the traditional husband–wife family household over the 1970s.

Table 2-7. Propensity for Homeownership by Household Type by Age, 1970 and 1980.

	Percentage Homeowners	
	1970	1980
Husband–wife family		
Less than 25	26.2	36.7
25–29	48.3	59.4
30–34	65.7	75.3
35–44	76.7	84.2
45–64	80.8	88.1
65 and over	78.4	84.9
Male-headed family (no wife)		
Under 65	49.1	45.3
65 and over	71.1	88.8
Female-headed family (no husband)		
Under 65	42.7	42.5
65 and over	69.9	73.2
Individual household		
Under 65	33.6	35.5
65 and over	54.1	58.9
All households	62.4*	64.7

Source: 1970 and 1980 censuses.

The basic life cycle and household type tenure tendencies are complemented by a set of economic determinants of tenure choice. The cost of homeownership relative to the cost of renting a housing unit is a critical factor. The current cost of owning a home is largely determined by the purchase price of the home and the mortgage interest rate, which together determine monthly mortgage payments. The annual property tax, maintenance and repair, and utility costs are also pertinent. In recent years additional items that tend to reduce the capital cost of homeownership have become increasingly important. These include (1) the deductibility for federal income tax purposes of property tax and mortgage interest payments and (2) the expected appreciation in the value of the housing unit.

The permanent or expected income of the household also has an important influence on the demand for ownership. Higher income households tend to have a greater demand for the space and privacy normally associated with owner-occupied units. In addition, the explicit and implicit tax subsidies to homeownership make this choice more desirable for high-income households. Because they are in higher tax brackets, the same actual expenses save them proportionately more money.

A final important short-run determinant of the effective demand for homeownership is the price and availability of mortgage credit. The price of mortgage credit is explicitly included in the cost of homeownership. Variation in mortgage interest rates has traditionally been considered one of the prime short-term determinants of new housing activity and the resale of existing homes. There seems to be complete agreement that, in the short run, increases in mortgage interest rates reduce the demand for mortgage credit and the number of housing starts and home sales. There are several channels, however, through which mortgage interest rates might affect the demand for homeownership. A change in the real mortgage rate (the mortgage rate minus the expected inflation rate) would be expected to have an inverse effect on demand. Even if the real mortgage rate is unchanged, a higher nominal rate raises mortgage payments immediately and would be expected to reduce the demand for housing. Another influence is the result of an expectations phenomenon. When mortgage interest rates rise, households might postpone a housing purchase in the expectation of lower mortgage rates in the future.

A second mortgage parameter that strongly influences housing demand is the down payment requirement. The initial down payment influences housing demand through a wealth effect. Higher down payments may prevent families with little wealth from purchasing a house or force them to purchase a lower priced home. This assumes imperfect capital markets in which individuals cannot borrow more than a certain amount against expected future income to increase initial equity. The effect of the down payment on the monthly mortgage payment works in the opposite direction. Higher down payments reduce the size of monthly payments and tend to increase the demand for housing. In a world of perfect information and perfect capital markets, these effects would exactly counterbalance each other, and variation in down payment requirements would have no influence on homeownership demand. However, empirical evidence indicates that the wealth constraint effect of the down payment is the dominant force.

The supply of mortgage credit also critically influences the short-run demand for homeownership. The short-run cyclical sensitivity of the housing market is largely the result of credit rationing, which periodically afflicts the housing market. During these periods the incremental demand for homeownership is drastically reduced, as the household is unable to obtain a mortgage loan at the prevailing mortgage interest rate.

In the past decade these forces have had contradictory influences on the homeownership rate. As mentioned above, the homeownership rate has increased significantly for traditional family households. Larger increases seem to be associated with younger families, but even the oldest husband–wife group stepped up its homeownership rate by almost five percentage points.

In contrast, factoring in single-parent families and individual households, the overall proportion of homeowners has risen only 0.6 percent. This aggregate result arises from the fact that the proportion of nontraditional households has, as previously shown, risen substantially. This latter type of household has a much lower proportion of homeowners. Since the overall homeownership proportion is an average of the traditional and nontraditional household homeownership rates, the growth in the share of non-traditional households has partially offset the growing propensity of husband–wife families to become homeowners. The net effect has produced only a modest increase in homeownership rates.

A continued trend toward homeownership in each household type and age category is expected for the 1980s despite the expectation of a continuing affordability problem for first-time buyers (see Chapter 7 for a full discussion of this). High relative house prices, continued high real mortgage interest rates, and high down payment requirements will continue to make it difficult for first-time buyers to enter the market. The continued strong investment appeal of owner-occupied housing and the likelihood of federal policy initiatives to assist the first-time buyer will counterbalance these constraints. However, from 1980–1982 the severe economic recession produced the first decline in homeownership in 50 years.

We view this decline as temporary. The strong economic incentives for homeownership when combined with an aging population showing proclivities to form primary family rather than individual households, will cause a sharp rise in the aggregate homeownership rate—possibly a rise to nearly 70 percent by 1990.

THE GEOGRAPHIC DISTRIBUTION OF HOUSING DEMAND

The major distinction between aggregate and regional analysis of housing markets is produced by the critical role of interregional migration. Policymakers must pay attention to differential migration rates. The type and cost of housing available in a region influence, but rarely control, migration decisions. Because surplus housing in one area is not readily transferable to others, examination of aggregate demand and supply figures can mask significant regional imbalances.

A region can be thought of as a metropolitan area, a state, or a group of states. While there may be good empirical and theoretical reasons for choosing a specific classification, the available data limit most annual analysis to a state basis or to a broad four-region basis, which is classified by the Census Bureau as Northeast, North Central, South, and West.

In the past decade there have been major differences in the rate of population growth between regions. Table 2–8 highlights the various components of this population growth. The Northeast has shown virtually no change in

Table 2-8.   Components of Population Change.[a]

Division and State	April 1, 1970 to April 1, 1980					April 1, 1980 to July 1, 1981				
	Net Change				Net Total Migra-	Net Change				Net Total Migra-
	Num-ber	Per-cent[b]	Births	Deaths	tion[c]	Num-ber	Per-cent[b]	Births	Deaths	tion[c]
United States	23,203	11.4	33,244	19,279	9,238	2,802	1.2	4,495	2,482	789
New England	501	4.2	1,607	1,135	29	96	.8	198	141	38
Maine	131	13.2	161	107	76	8	.7	20	13	1
New Hampshire	183	24.8	122	75	136	15	1.6	17	9	7
Vermont	67	15.0	72	44	38	4	.8	10	6	(Z)*
Massachusetts	48	.8	737	553	136	36	.6	88	67	16
Rhode Island	− 3	− .3	123	93	− 33	6	.6	15	12	2
Connecticut	75	2.5	391	263	− 52	26	.8	48	33	11
Middle Atlantic	425	1.1	5,055	3,534	− 1,946	88	.2	616	455	− 73
New York	684	3.8	2,481	1,622	− 1,543	44	.3	298	215	− 39
New Jersey	193	2.7	981	674	− 114	40	.5	120	86	5
Pennsylvania	66	.6	1,593	1,238	− 289	4	(Z)	197	154	− 39
East North Central	1,407	3.5	6,454	3,723	1,324	− 14	(− Z)	835	458	− 391
Ohio	140	1.3	1,676	992	− 544	− 17	.2	215	126	− 105
Indiana	295	5.7	865	483	− 87	− 22	− .4	110	59	− 73
Illinois	308	2.8	1,790	1,072	− 410	43	.4	237	128	− 66
Michigan	377	4.2	1,441	767	− 297	− 54	.6	181	94	− 141
Wisconsin	288	6.5	682	408	14	36	.8	93	51	− 6
West North Central	857	5.2	2,579	1,617	− 105	53	.3	352	194	− 105
Minnesota	271	7.1	595	334	11	17	.4	81	39	− 25
Iowa	88	3.1	432	286	− 58	− 15	− .5	58	33	− 40
Missouri	240	5.1	728	505	16	23	.5	98	62	− 13
North Dakota	35	5.6	107	56	− 17	6	.9	15	7	− 2
South Dakota	24	3.6	117	66	− 26	− 5	− .7	16	8	− 13
Nebraska	85	5.7	246	149	− 12	7	.4	34	18	− 9
Kansas	114	5.1	354	221	19	19	.8	51	27	− 4
South Atlantic	6,264	20.4	5,149	3,088	4,204	808	2.2	685	413	536
Delaware	47	8.6	88	49	8	3	.5	12	6	− 2
Maryland	293	7.5	568	331	55	47	1.1	75	43	15
Dist. of Columbia	− 119	− 15.7	109	77	− 151	− 7	− 1.1	12	9	− 10
Virginia	695	14.9	748	406	353	83	1.6	98	53	39
West Virginia	205	11.8	290	198	113	2	.1	36	24	− 10
North Carolina	790	15.5	863	468	395	79	1.3	106	61	34
South Carolina	528	20.4	498	241	272	48	1.5	65	31	14
Georgia	876	19.1	862	429	443	109	2.0	116	55	49
Florida	2,949	43.4	1,121	889	2,716	443	4.5	165	130	408
East South Central	1,855	14.5	2,301	1,309	863	60	.4	299	166	− 72
Kentucky	441	13.7	568	336	209	1	(Z)	74	42	− 31
Tennessee	665	16.9	664	393	394	21	.5	86	51	− 14
Alabama	446	12.9	615	346	176	27	.7	80	44	− 8
Mississippi	304	13.7	454	235	85	10	.4	59	29	− 19
West South Central	4,417	22.9	3,772	1,848	2,493	727	3.1	555	243	415
Arkansas	362	18.8	349	218	232	10	.4	46	28	− 8
Louisiana	559	15.3	717	346	188	104	2.5	103	44	45
Oklahoma	466	18.2	445	274	295	75	2.5	65	35	46
Texas	3,030	27.1	2,261	1,010	1,779	538	3.8	340	135	333

Table 2-8.   (Continued)

Division and State	April 1, 1970 to April 1, 1980					April 1, 1980 to July 1, 1981				
	Net Change				Net Total Migra-tion[c]	Net Change				Net Total Migra-tion[c]
	Num-ber	Per-cent[b]	Births	Deaths		Num-ber	Per-cent[b]	Births	Deaths	
Mountain	3,078	37.1	1,837	722	1,963	326	2.9	281	101	145
Montana	92	13.3	126	67	33	6	.7	18	8	− 3
Idaho	231	32.4	166	65	130	15	1.6	25	8	− 1
Wyoming	138	41.6	73	31	96	21	4.5	13	4	12
Colorado	679	30.7	415	182	446	76	2.6	62	24	38
New Mexico	283	27.8	224	82	141	28	2.1	33	11	6
Arizona	942	53.1	405	174	712	76	2.8	62	27	41
Utah	402	37.9	329	76	149	57	3.9	52	10	15
Nevada	310	63.5	99	46	257	46	5.7	17	9	− 37
Pacific	5,249	19.8	4,493	2,305	3,060	659	2.1	674	310	295
Washington	717	21.0	548	305	474	87	2.1	84	40	44
Oregon	541	25.9	351	207	396	18	.7	53	27	− 8
California	3,697	18.5	3,354	1,734	2,078	527	2.2	502	234	260
Alaska	98	32.4	78	15	36	11	2.8	12	2	2
Hawaii	195	25.3	163	44	76	16	1.6	23	6	− 1

[a] In thousands, except percent.

[b] 1970 to 1980 based on 1970 population, 1980 to 1981 based on 1980 population.

[c] Comprises net immigration from abroad, net interdivisional or interstate migration, movement of persons in the Armed Forces, and the "error of closure."

* (Z) indicates less than 500 or .05 percent.

Source: U.S. Bureau of the Census, *Current Population Reports,* series P-25, No. 911, and unpublished data.

population between 1970 and 1980. The North Central had a slow 4 percent increase. The South and West, however, experienced massive population increases of 20 percent and nearly 24 percent, respectively.

There is even more divergence within regions. In the Northeast, New York lost population, while New Hampshire registered a 25 percent gain in population. All North Central region states tallied small gains, ranging from 1.3 percent in Ohio to over 7 percent in Minnesota. All southern states showed substantial gains, with Texas (27.1%) and Florida (43.4%) leading the way. In the West, California added nearly 3.7 million people (18.5%), but the highest rates of increase occurred in Wyoming (41.6%), Arizona (53.1%), and Nevada (53.5%).

While there are statistically significant variations in birth and death rates in different areas, the major cause of these substantial differences is migration. A number of academic and research papers have examined this process, finding that interregional migration is primarily driven by employment and earnings differentials. This is especially true for the working-age population, for which differences in unemployment rates and real income (income adjusted for the local cost of living) explain over three-fourths of the variance in interstate migration rates. For the retirement-age population, and increasingly for the working-age population, environmental amenities such as a warm climate, access to recreational opportunities, and lower population densities are becoming a more significant part of migration decisions.

Differential population growth is the major cause of differential housing demand by region, but there are also regional variations in the rate of household formation from a given population. The West has significantly higher rates of individual household formation than the rest of the country, primarily because of the higher divorce rate in this region. Also, there are substantial regional variations in the proportion of households that choose to own rather than rent (see Table 2-9). The North Central region shows significantly higher rates of homeownership, the Northeast significantly lower ones. Different homeownership propensities primarily reflect historic differentials in the cost of homeownership. The recent surge in house prices in the West would be expected to reduce homeownership in that region.

Policymakers must also take into consideration the central-city–suburban distribution of activity, which is critically influenced by the intrametropoli-

Table 2-9. Owner-Occupied Units and Homeownership by Age and Type of Household by Region, 1980.

	Northeast		North Central		South		West	
Husband owner	9,010	(67.9)	10,674	(83.4)	12,616	(79.6)	6,680	(62.8)
Under 25	102	(29.2)	308	(40.6)	393	(39.3)	137	(30.3)
25–34	1,391	(65.5)	2,307	(74.2)	2,640	(68.6)	1,303	(59.9)
35–64	4,860	(83.8)	6,413	(90.6)	7,481	(86.9)	4,094	(84.2)
65 and over	1,186	(76.2)	1,646	(88.7)	2,104	(87.5)	1,146	(85.1)
Other male headship	431	(48.2)	513	(52.1)	604	(48.2)	479	(42.3)
Under 65	336	(44.4)	418	(47.9)	469	(43.4)	428	(40.4)
65 and over	95	(68.8)	95	(84.8)	136	(78.6)	50	(70.4)
Female headship	1,041	(41.0)	1,250	(49.3)	1,890	(51.4)	845	(42.6)
Under 65	766	(35.6)	989	(45.2)	1,438	(46.8)	728	(40.0)
65 and over	274	(70.3)	261	(74.4)	452	(74.7)	117	(71.8)
Single person household	1,470	(36.8)	2,178	(48.2)	2,837	(51.6)	1,469	(39.4)
Under 65	668	(33.0)	983	(38.5)	1,313	(41.1)	803	(31.8)
65 and over	802	(49.9)	1,196	(60.7)	1,524	(66.2)	667	(55.4)
All households	10,480	(60.7)	14,616	(70.1)	17,948	(68.3)	9,472	(60.4)

Source: U.S. Bureau of the Census.

tan migration decisions. Census data show that over 80 percent of moves within a metropolitan area are motivated by the desire to improve housing and neighborhood conditions. Traditional economic theory has emphasized to an extreme the critical role of the journey to work in determining the intrametropolitan location of a household. The "theory of the local public sector" has emphasized the role of the tax rates and local public services in determining household location: households are seen to "vote with their feet" as they move among jurisdictions, seeking the optimum available package of services and taxes. A complete theory of household location decisions would include access to workplace, shopping, and recreation; tax cost and local services received; and neighborhood factors such as race, income, ethnicity, and physical amenities.

The effects of this array of variables on households depends largely on the characteristics of the household involved. Much of the theoretical and empirical literature assumes a homogeneous household, the exceptions giving some consideration to differing racial and income characteristics. The fundamental restructuring of the American household discussed earlier might make some of the traditional findings and relationships less relevant to the present situation. The single, divorced, or childless couple is likely to have very different location preferences than the traditional husband, wife, and two-children household. If both spouses are working, even the traditional household might have a changed set of location preferences relative to the one-worker family.

The post–World War II suburbanization of the traditional household has been attributed to the improvement of the intrametropolitan highway system, the provision of government-insured mortgage loans, and the physical and fiscal benefits of suburban jurisdictions. Recently, a number of these forces have begun to work in a different direction. Congestion and the sharp rise in gasoline prices have increased the time and money costs of transportation to central business district employment from suburban locations. Suburban house prices have soared. Government policies have been retargeted to aid ailing central cities. There has been a boom in the construction of center-city office space and white collar job creation. These and other factors have made centrally located housing relatively more attractive. Empirical evidence on these trends is just becoming available, but the AHS does provide a clear view of historic differences between central-city and suburban housing markets. (See Table 2–10.)

Central cities have a much higher proportion of individual and young households, a lower proportion of homeowners, a higher proportion of poor and black households, and a lower cost of housing. Individual households make up nearly one-fourth of households in the central city, while husband–wife family households make up only one-half of all central-city households. In the suburbs the husband–wife family household is by far the

Table 2-10. Central-City and Suburban Housing.

	Central City		Suburbs	
	1980	1970	1980	1970
Proportion owner-occupied	49.5	48.1	70.9	70.3
Total occupied housing units	23,832	21,395	30,718	22,464
Husband–wife	11,170 (46.8)	12,704 (59.4)	19,707 (64.2)	16,895 (75.2)
Other male head	1,484 (6.2)	959 (4.5)	1,693 (5.5)	753 (3.4)
Female head	4,257 (17.9)	2,817 (16.0)	3,686 (12.0)	1,799 (8.0)
Single person	6,919 (29.0)	4,916 (23.0)	5,631 (18.3)	3,017 (13.4)
Median income owner-occupied units	19,500	10,100	23,500	11,600
Median income renter-occupied units	9,800	6,100	12,400	7,700
Proportion of black households	5,073 (21.3)	3,833 (17.9)	1,696 (5.5)	906 (4.0)

Source: Raw data from *Annual Housing Survey*.

dominant element, making up 75 percent of all suburban household units. The income of the typical suburban household is between 20 and 35 percent higher than that of the corresponding central-city household. Furthermore, the proportion of black households in the central city is nearly five times that in suburban jurisdictions.

As a result of these differences in household composition, income, and race, central-city housing demand are characterized by a far lower proportion of homeownership than suburban areas. Only half of central-city households own their own homes, as compared with over 70 percent in the suburbs, but the proportion of homeowners has been increasing more rapidly in central cities than in suburban areas since 1970.

The deterioration of central-city housing markets, which has occurred rapidly for over two decades, shows some evidence of reversing itself in a number of metropolitan areas in the 1980s. The concept of the "city as sandbox," which became a popular vision in the late 1960s and early 1970s, has changed significantly. A number of cities are now confronted with tight housing markets (low vacancy rates), displacement, and gentrification—all resulting from the revitalization of the city as a workplace and living environment. While there is much variation in this trend, it appears that a number of cities—for example, New York (specifically, Manhattan), San Francisco, Boston, Washington, D.C., Seattle, and Minneapolis—have a vibrant future in the 1980s. On the other hand, Buffalo, St. Louis, Newark, and Cleveland are far from achieving a recovery in the 1980s.

In terms of interregional migration, trends of the late 1970s are not necessarily good indicators for the 1980s. States that are net energy exporters will no longer gain population and income at the expense of net importers. The general movement to the South and West should continue, though at a slower rate, reflecting both job opportunities and environmental amenities. Even an attempt to reindustrialize the U.S. economy will not alter these basic trends, as reindustrialization may well encourage new capital formation in the Sun Belt. There are, again, exceptions. The long period of New England's relative decline appears to have ended. Massive defense spending and the development of the electronics and information service industries should put this area on a high-growth path. In the North Central region, Wisconsin and Minnesota appear surprisingly strong. In the West and South, states such as Montana and Mississippi do not appear to be especially vibrant. In addition, Houston, the most vibrant growth area of the 1970s, appears to be a likely five-star loser city through at least the mid-1980s. Houston's problems result from the energy glut, the collapse of the export of capital from Mexico, the failure to plan adequately for infrastructure needs, and the large overbuilding boom of the early 1980s. Despite these few exceptions, the broad interregional migration trends of the late 1970s should continue into the 1980s.

More accurate specific forecasts of the housing situation in individual regions can be obtained by applying the methodology developed in the first part of this chapter to the demographic and economic environment of particular areas. For the nation as a whole, however, the picture is clear. Substantial increments to the national housing stock are required if the long-standing American dream of homeownership is to be accommodated in the 1980s.

NOTES

1. Key studies are summarized in "Estimates of Housing Needs 1975–1980," Committee on Banking, Housing, and Urban Affairs (Washington, D.C., Government Printing Office, 1975).

2. Tiebout, C.M. "A Pure Theory of Local Expenditures," *Journal of Political Economy,* 65, no. 5 (October 1956), 416–424.

3. This comparison uses the homeownership component of the CPI, which is not adjusted for tax benefits or capital appreciation realized or expected by homeowners. Accordingly, it tends to overstate the actual cost of homeownership.

4. $hh_{ijt} = f(Y_{ijt}, R_t, D_t)$

This relationship merely states that households of type i are formed within age group j at time t at a rate that is determined by real income (Y_{ijt}), the relative cost of rental housing (R_t), and the prevailing divorce rate (D_t) as a proxy for all sociological forces.

Historical data have been used elsewhere to estimate and verify this relationship. Separation equations were identified for each age group and household type. These relationships can then be combined with forecasts of income, rental costs, and divorce rates to predict household headship rates for the 1980s.

Chapter 3

The Supply and Demand for Mortgage Credit

SUPPLY OF MORTGAGE FUNDS

The availability and price of mortgage credit critically influence the ability of those involved in the housing market to actualize underlying demand and supply preferences. The mortgage market has to be discussed and analyzed for the most part in national terms because regional and intrametropolitan effects are largely nonexistent due to the highly fungible nature of financial credit. This examination therefore focuses on private, institutional sources of mortgage credits; the role of government housing finance agencies is examined in Chapter 6.

The residential mortgage loan is the major instrument of housing finance. A mortgage is a loan to the purchaser of a parcel of real estate to cover a portion of its cost. In return for the loan, the lender receives an interest in the property as collateral and a schedule for the payment of interest and re-payment of the original amount of the loan or principal. Until the early 1980s nearly all residential mortgage loans made were "fully amortized" with a mortgage interest rate and payments that were fixed for the term of the loan. This means that the interest and principal are paid off in equal, periodic installments, with the entire debt discharged by the time of its maturity. Since 1981 there has been a major restructuring of the mortgage instrument, which will be discussed in Chapter 7.

Widespread use of the fully amortized residential mortgage loan is primarily a post–Great Depression phenomenon. In the 1920s only about 15 percent of home mortgages were fully amortized, half were partially amortized, and the remainder were due and payable in a lump sum at the time of maturity. In practice, nonamortized loans were automatically refinanced and repayment of the principal could be delayed indefinitely.

In the past seventy-five years there have been major changes in the housing finance system. A large increase in the use of debt financing has emerged; the system has become largely institutionalized, with financial intermediaries rather than households extending the vast majority of loans (even though the creative financing surge from 1980 to 1982 represented a temporary shift in this trend); and the federal government has come to play a growing role, through indirect insurance of loans and directly through the provision of loans and advances to private mortgage originators.

The high capital costs and extreme durability of housing make debt financing necessary and attractive. The fact that housing has a long useful economic life means that the services a housing unit provides in any one year are small compared with the services provided over its entire economic life. Since current household income is small in comparison to the total cost of the unit, the household must rely heavily on borrowing to purchase housing unless it has managed to save substantial amounts of money during previous years.

American reliance on mortgage borrowing for the acquisition of housing has increased substantially over time. In 1915 the average household borrowed only about half the value of the dwelling unit. At present some 70 to 80 percent of housing purchase costs are financed through a mortgage loan. This increase in the use of mortgage debt has come about as a result of changes in attitudes of consumers and lenders and the growing importance of financial intermediaries as the focus of savings and lending activity.

There has been a substantial change in consumer and lender attitudes toward the assumption of all types of debt, including mortgage loans. The increased acceptance of the borrowing philosophy is especially characteristic of the purchase of durable goods such as housing. It reflects a growing acceptance of borrowing for the purchase of goods and services desired now and affordable only in the future.

In addition, the Federal Housing Administration (FHA) and Veterans' Administration (VA) government mortgage insurance and assistance programs have encouraged the use of borrowing to purchase housing. The low, and often negligible, down payment requirements of these government plans have also encouraged the non-government-assisted market to increase loan-to-value ratios. On average, only about 15 percent of homes are purchased without borrowing. For the other 85 percent an average of 75 percent of the purchase price is financed. A substantial number of first-time buyers may borrow 90 to 95 percent of the value of their homes.

Another major alteration in the housing finance system has been the institutionalization of the provision of mortgage loans. Table 3–1 shows that in the early 1900s nearly 50 percent of all mortgages were provided by the

Table 3-1. Percentage Distribution of Nonfarm Residential Mortgage Debt Outstanding by Type of Holder.

Year	Non-institutional[a]	Savings and Loan Associations	Mutual Savings Banks	Commercial Banks	Life Insurance Companies	Sponsored Credit Agencies[b]	Other[c]
1905	45.5	12.7	23.4	8.3	7.2	—	2.9
1915	37.0	18.3	23.5	9.4	8.7	—	3.1
1925	37.5	23.2	17.6	10.8	8.2	—	2.7
1935	31.4	14.9	17.9	10.0	9.9	—	15.9
1945	32.0	20.9	13.7	13.8	14.7	—	4.9
1955	10.0	34.0	12.6	17.1	20.0	—	6.3
1965	5.5	44.2	14.1	14.3	13.9	1.2	—
1970	4.6	44.6	13.3	15.1	9.5	5.7	—
1975	7.6	45.6	10.2	15.7	3.6	12.4	—
1980	8.0	43.7	6.8	16.7	1.9	17.2	5.7

a Individual households account for the bulk of noninstitutional mortgage holding.

b Includes GNMA.

c Includes holdings of federal government (especially the Home Owners' Loan Corporation during and after the depression), state, and local governments; credit unions; private pension funds; finance companies; and real estate investment trusts.

Sources: 1905–45 data from Leo Grebler, David Blank, and Louis Winnick, *Capital Formation in Residential Real Estate* (Princeton, N.J.: Princeton University Press, 1956), pp. 472–74; 1955–74 data from Federal Reserve Board System, *Flow of Funds Accounts*.

previous owner of a property to its new purchaser. By 1979, however, the share of residential mortgages outstanding held by such households had declined to 7.5 percent. From 1980 to 1982, the share of household mortgages outstanding rose slightly, reflecting the holding of "seller second" mortgages. However, in 1983 and 1984, the public and private "financial intermediaries"—so called because they are interposed between the buyer and seller of a property—are again providing the bulk of mortgage financing. This trend toward institutionalization is not confined to mortgage financing. It is primarily because of the tremendous institutionalization of all personal savings that the financial intermediaries have become so large a part of the mortgage market. Private financial intermediaries involved heavily in mortgage finance have conventionally been grouped into four classes: savings and loan associations (SLAs), mutual savings banks (MSBs), commercial banks (CBs), and life insurance companies (LICs). SLAs and MSBs are collectively designated "thrift institutions."

Government insurance (FHA and VA) programs have facilitated intermediary participation in the mortgage market. They have helped to standardize lending criteria and improve marketability of the mortgage. Greater participation by some of these intermediaries has also been encouraged by the gradual liberalization of legal restrictions on the asset portfolios of these institutions. These reductions in restrictions have been especially important to CBs and LICs. Table 3–1 provides an indication of the accelerated reliance on borrowing and the changing roles of these various credit sources. The significance of mortgages to private intermediaries on an absolute basis and as a percentage of their asset portfolio is demonstrated in Table 3–2.

Traditional Mortgage Lenders

Savings and Loan Associations.   SLAs became the dominant source of credit in the residential finance market as a result of government regulations and superior market performance. Since the early part of this century, the SLA mortgage market share has almost quadrupled; by 1982 they held over 40 percent of all residential mortgages outstanding in their asset portfolios. Total SLA assets grew from $8.7 billion in 1945 to over $706 billion in 1982. During the period from the end of World War II to 1965 these associations experienced nearly uninterrupted double-digit growth rates. Since 1965 SLA expansion has slowed considerably, with especially poor performances during the credit crunches of 1966, 1969, 1974, 1980, and 1982.

This rapid growth was primarily the result of the superior ability of SLAs to attract personal savings deposits. Federal deposit regulations (discussed below) provided a comparative advantage to thrift institutions. Since SLAs specialized nearly exclusively in residential real estate loans because of portfolio restrictions, most of this large increment of savings deposits was chan-

Table 3-2. Mortgage Assets of Financial Intermediaries (in $ billions) and (in percentages).

Year	Savings and Loan Associations	Mutual Savings Banks	Life Insurance Companies	Commercial Banks
1905	0.4 (N/A)[a]	0.9 (26.6)	0.3 (9.4)	0.3 (1.1)
1915	1.1 (N/A)[a]	1.4 (32.1)	0.5 (10.1)	0.6 (2.1)
1925	4.0 (86.4)	3.0 (37.8)	1.4 (12.2)	1.8 (3.2)
1935	3.3 (N/A)[a]	4.0 (35.7)	2.2 (9.5)	2.1 (3.9)
1945	6.1 (69.5)	3.4 (19.9)	3.7 (8.1)	3.4 (2.1)
1955	30.6 (81.3)	15.6 (49.7)	21.2 (24.1)	15.9 (8.6)
1965	102.4 (79.0)	40.1 (68.8)	38.4 (24.9)	32.4 (9.6)
1975	249.4 (73.7)	63.8 (52.7)	37.2 (13.3)	83.1 (9.4)
1980	457.9 (72.6)	83.5 (48.7)	37.5 (7.8)	173.2 (11.2)
1982	436.3 (61.8)	78.7 (45.1)	36.1 (6.2)	193.0 (10.6)

[a] Indicates that total asset figures are not available.

Note: Figures in parentheses are the percentage of total assets reflected by mortgages.

Sources: 1905–45, Grebler, Blank, and Winnick, *Capital Formation in Residential Real Estate,* pp. 481–85; 1955–74, Federal Reserve System, *Flow of Funds Accounts*; 1905–35, Raymond W. Goldsmith, *A Study of Saving in the United States,* vol. 1 (Princeton: Princeton University Press, 1955).

neled in that direction. Some 70 percent of SLA assets have gone to the provision of real estate credit. The remainder of their asset portfolio has been held primarily in government securities, demand deposits, and currency to provide needed liquidity.

The mortgage holdings of SLAs are primarily non-government-insured conventional loans. Despite a typical contractual term of thirty years, these loans have had an average life of only twelve years because of prepayment and refinancing of mortgages. This is still quite a long time in comparison to the average term of SLA liabilities. By mid-1984 more than half of newly originated loans by SLAs were adjustable rate mortgages, thus reducing the asset-liability mismatch at least at the margin.

On the liability side, the SLAs primarily hold personal savings deposits. The remainder of their liability portfolio is composed primarily of advances (loans) from the Federal Home Loan Bank Board (FHLBB). Until about 1969 the majority of these savings were in passbook accounts that could be withdrawn by depositors at any time. From 1969 to 1978 SLAs made attempts to lengthen the maturity of their liabilities. By offering higher yielding certificates of deposit they hoped to attract and lock in longer maturity deposits and so reduce cash management problems. By 1977 nearly 60 percent of deposits were in these certificate accounts. Introduction of the money market certificate (MMC) in 1978 and the money market deposit accounts (MMDA) in 1982 brought progress in lengthening liability maturity to a halt: by mid-1984 nearly 75 percent of deposits were in short-term, "hot money" certificates or deposits.

Lengthening the maturity structure of liabilities is potentially of great importance to the continued viability of the SLAs. The major problem they have faced in the past ten years has been a result of their portfolio imbalance: "borrowing short" and "lending long." When the normal yield relationship (short-term rates lower than long-term rates) inverted, SLAs faced substantial cash flow and liquidity difficulties. By attempting to lengthen the maturity of their liabilities the SLAs hoped to achieve a better matching of their asset and liability portfolios, reducing the difficulties caused by the frequent yield curve inversions of the past ten years. Unfortunately, the recent money market accounts have substantially worsened the maturity imbalance problem. On the other hand, widespread use of variable rate mortgages could, over time, lessen the maturity imbalance problem.

Historically, a major cause of the maturity imbalance problem was government regulations on deposit interest rates. Regulation Q placed a ceiling on interest rates payable for passbook accounts and certificates of deposits by mortgage providers. Thrift institutions were permitted to pay somewhat higher rates (the "differential") under the terms of this regulation. Actual interest rates paid were determined by market forces until they reached Regulation Q ceilings.

These provisions were initially applied to SLAs during their liquidity crisis of 1966, although they had been applied to CBs since the early 1930s. It was hoped that, by forcing a uniform rate differential between SLAs and CBs, the outflow of funds from SLAs ("disintermediation") would be stemmed and mortgage lending encouraged because of the mandated specialization of SLAs in this area. These controls were meant to be a temporary emergency measure, but they persisted. Their initial purpose of preventing interest rate competition from other deposit-taking institutions was partially achieved, but they failed to solve the problem of fund outflows because of their inability to control interest rates offered by nonregulated competitors. During the past two credit crunches open capital market rates rose substantially above Regulation Q ceilings. This led to massive disintermediation (withdrawal of funds) from all traditional depository institutions attracted by higher returns offered by the open capital market and money market mutual funds. This disintermediation from SLAs in turn led to a scarcity of mortgage funds and a sharp curtailment of lending for housing purchases.

Since the middle of 1978 major modifications in Regulation Q ceilings have allowed financial institutions more flexibility in meeting the disintermediation problem. In June 1978 the regulations on savings deposit interest rate ceilings were changed to allow thrift institutions and CBs to issue a six-month certificate, with the ceiling rate determined by the rate that prevailed at the most recent auction of six-month Treasury bills. SLAs (and MSBs) were allowed to pay 0.25 percent differential over the CB rate. In January 1980 a longer term (thirty-month) instrument tied to the three- to five-year Treasury bond rate was authorized. This "small saver certificate" (SSC) was meant to allow lower income households to receive returns closer to market rates. The most significant deregulation occurred in December 1982, when depository institutions were allowed to issue money market deposit accounts (MMDAs) with no interest rate ceilings. This new account represented the de facto end of Regulation Q ceilings.

The deregulation prior to 1982 was moderately successful at preserving the flow of deposit funds to financial institutions during tight money periods. However, the SLA experience of 1980–82 indicates that this type of liability structure has not resolved the mortgage credit supply problem. SLA deposits in 1980–82 were down substantially from the preceding years, and SLAs experienced an earnings crisis that threatened their continued existence as mortgage lenders. While the impact of the MMDA in 1983 has been extremely positive in terms of deposit flows and mortgage lending, the maturity imbalance problem of SLAs is far from solved.

Mutual Savings Banks. In the early 1900s MSBs were the largest institutional source of residential mortgages. Since that time their share of the mortgage market has substantially declined. At present they hold about 6.8 percent of residential mortgages outstanding. This reduction in market share is not due to a decreased specialization in the residential mortgage market. On the contrary, Table 3-2 shows that the share of MSB assets invested in mortgages has doubled since the early years of this century. The major reason for their relative decline in importance to the mortgage market is the regional shift in population growth away from areas in which MSBs are geographically concentrated: the Northeast and the Middle Atlantic States. Since much of the population and housing stock growth in the past fifty years has been concentrated in the southern and western regions, the ability of MSBs to attract savings and pursue mortgage investment opportunities has diminished relative to more geographically dispersed financial intermediaries.

MSBs were less constrained by regulation than were SLAs. Portfolio allocations were determined more by management than by government. This increased flexibility allowed them to take advantage of market opportunities and achieve a more balanced matching of asset and liability maturities. However, usury law ceilings in New York and New Jersey, major MSB states, provided substantial distortions in their asset portfolios. On the liability side, MSBs faced Regulation Q provisions on ceiling interest rates by account type similar to those faced by SLAs. For this reason MSBs faced similar, periodic disintermediation and earning crises. Despite recent deregulations, MSBs will not play a major role in the future of housing finance.

Commercial Banks.   The CB share of the mortgage market has doubled since the early 1900s. By 1982 the commercial banking system held the second-largest portfolio of mortgages among private depository institutions — $193 billion of mortgage assets, constituting nearly 17 percent of all residential mortgages.

The main reason for the increased penetration of the mortgage market by CBs is a shift in their portfolio allocation toward residential mortgages. As shown in Table 3–2, CBs now allocate close to 11 percent of their portfolio to residential mortgages, whereas only 2 to 4 percent was allocated in the pre–World War II period. This portfolio diversification has been attributed to a gradual lifting of previous federal and state restrictions on bank lending to the real estate market. Within the constraints imposed by cash reserve requirements, CBs are able to allocate their assets in accordance with prudent management goals.

However, the interest rates they are allowed to pay on accounts of various maturities and size were also limited under the provisions of Regulation Q. The deregulation of deposit accounts, which culminated with the introduction of the MMDA, provides CBs with the most promising future as financial intermediaries and mortgage lenders. The previous lack of restrictions on their asset structure has provided them with the best asset-liability matching of any financial intermediary. They are thus best able to deal with the extreme interest rate volatility of the 1980s.

Life Insurance Companies.   LICs have played a mixed role in the residential mortgage market. Their share of loans outstanding rose from 7 percent at the beginning of the century to over 20 percent at its peak in the mid-1950s. Since then their role has diminished. At present they hold less than 2 percent of loans outstanding, their lowest relative share in the residential mortgage market this century.

This long-term variation in market share is due to fluctuations in their rate of asset growth and in the allocation of those assets. After World War II, LICs dramatically shifted their assets to the mortgage market. Their residential mortgage holdings expanded from 10 to nearly 25 percent of their assets due to acquisition of a large portion of government-backed mortgages originated during the postwar housing boom. Since the mid-1960s the mortgage interest rate has fallen relative to the return on other assets, leading LICs virtually to cease making single-family mortgage loans and confine their role to lending to the commercial sector and to equity participation in commercial real estate.

This portfolio shift has been accentuated by the decline in LIC asset expansion caused by the virtual explosion in the growth of private pension funds, which are a substitute for savings held in life insurance policies. The net effect of these changes is that LICs are no longer one of the major forces in the residential mortgage market. Despite an asset increase of $340 billion in the past ten years, their residential mortgage holdings actually decreased over $1 billion.

Recent Trends in Mortgage Supply by Traditional Lenders[1]

While these depository institutions have become the predominant lenders in terms of their share of total mortgage originations and total mortgage holdings, there have been some recent changes in these trends. The share of mortgages held by thrift institutions declined by ten percentage points from 1977 to 1982. As Table 3-3 shows, CB holdings have remained stable, and

Table 3-3.   Share of Total Mortgages Held.

Year	Savings and Loan Associations	Mutual Savings Banks	Commercial Banks	Insurance Companies	Mortgage Companies
1970	.458	.157	.148	.097	.022
1971	.473	.148	.149	.081	.021
1972	.493	.140	.155	.066	.019
1973	.502	.133	.164	.054	.013
1974	.499	.124	.169	.047	.009
1975	.503	.114	.165	.039	.009
1976	.514	.107	.164	.031	.009
1977	.519	.099	.167	.024	.009
1978	.507	.092	.174	.020	.011
1979	.486	.085	.175	.020	.013
1980	.478	.080	.171	.020	.008
1981	.465	.074	.170	.018	.007
1982	.415	.071	.166	.017	.007

Source: Department of Housing and Urban Development.

LIC and MSB holdings have continued to decline. The share of all mortgages held by depository institutions declined by almost 25 percent over this brief period. This large reduction in the institutional holding of mortgages has had a dramatic impact on the housing finance system.

Table 3-4. Share of Total Mortgage Originations.

Year	Savings and Loan Associations	Mutual Savings Banks	Commercial Banks	Insurance Companies	Mortgage Companies
1970	.416	.060	.219	.009	.250
1971	.460	.061	.218	.006	.216
1972	.484	.067	.233	.005	.176
1973	.486	.075	.237	.005	.160
1974	.458	.058	.239	.005	.193
1975	.529	.056	.185	.003	.180
1976	.549	.057	.217	.003	.140
1977	.533	.053	.226	.003	.158
1978	.486	.051	.237	.005	.186
1979	.444	.048	.218	.011	.243
1980	.457	.041	.215	.013	.220
1981	.427	.041	.221	.005	.244
1982	.366	.042	.245	.006	.295

Source: Department of Housing and Urban Development.

Table 3-5. Share of New Home, Mortgage Origination.

Year	Savings and Loan Associations	Mutual Savings Banks	Commercial Banks	Insurance Companies	Mortgage Companies
1970	.469	.048	.171	.014	.236
1971	.458	.035	.178	.008	.266
1972	.485	.036	.193	.009	.221
1973	.515	.047	.180	.006	.194
1974	.500	.038	.180	.005	.200
1975	.524	.033	.153	.002	.202
1976	.549	.039	.197	.003	.156
1977	.528	.035	.205	.003	.186
1978	.478	.030	.199	.004	.242
1979	.464	.026	.187	.016	.270
1980	.467	.023	.164	.020	.276
1981	.462	.024	.177	.005	.270
1982	.354	.026	.192	.007	.342

Source: Department of Housing and Urban Development.

Tables 3–4 and 3–5 show the annual total and new home mortgage origination shares since 1970 for depository institutions and mortgage companies. SLA shares have dropped sharply in the past five years. This is one reason there has been a sharp decline in the share of mortgages they hold. The other major reason is mortgage sales by SLAs to other entities. The sale of mortgages by SLAs was especially dramatic during the liquidity and profit squeeze of 1982. A similar pattern holds for MSBs. Their share of total mortgage originations is now under 4 percent, having declined steadily since 1973. Consistent with the stock level data, CB total mortgage origination shares have been comparatively stable since 1970, although recent figures suggest that CBs may be trending upward.

In contrast to both SLAs and CBs, the share of all mortgages originated by mortgage companies is rising rapidly. In 1982 mortgage companies originated nearly one-third of all mortgage loans, a substantial rise from their historic share. As Table 3–3 indicates, mortgage companies essentially sell all their mortgage loans. This dramatic increase in the mortgage company share of mortgages originated since 1976 is counterbalancing the decline in the thrift institution share.

Historically, the decline in mortgage market activity of thrift institutions has been caused by reductions in the size and stability of their deposit flows. Table 3–6 illustrates the situation for SLA deposit flows since 1970. Column (1) shows the ratio of new SLA deposits to the total volume of mortgage originations for all lenders. An especially large drop occurred in the key periods of disintermediation, such as 1970 and 1974, when open market rates exceeded Regulation Q ceilings, but the ratio rebounded the following year in both instances. Since 1977, however, there has been a distinct downtrend that appears secular, not cyclical. The pattern is similar when interest credited to SLAs is added to the numerator, but the ratio declines less dramatically because interest credited has been sharply rising because of higher interest rates. Similar ratios have been constructed using total national savings in the denominator. The patterns are the same, with a secular downtrend since 1977. Overall, SLAs have increasingly failed either to generate deposit flows that keep pace with total mortgage originations or to maintain their share of national savings. The introduction of the MMDA in late 1982 has dramatically reversed this downward trend in SLA deposit share. However, it is too soon to generalize from the experience of 1983. In addition to a reduction in market share, a rising share of SLA deposits have come in the form of "hot money"—short-term deposits—and the institutions have wisely been reluctant to commit these funds for investments in long-term mortgage assets. These same factors—the reduced magnitude of savings flows and the predominance of short-term deposits—have affected MSBs even more sharply.

Table 3-6. SLA Savings Flow Relative to Mortgage Originations and National Savings.

Year	(1)[a]	(2)[b]	(3)[c]	(4)[d]
1970	.149	.305	.095	.194
1971	.357	.473	.341	.451
1972	.315	.421	.454	.607
1973	.133	.252	.133	.753
1974	.069	.231	.055	.183
1975	.376	.540	.311	.446
1976	.305	.441	.417	.603
1977	.198	.310	.410	.644
1978	.127	.239	.263	.494
1979	.081	.208	.155	.402
1980	.080	.306	.100	.386
1981	−.259	.137	−.195	.103
1982	−.068	.393	−.045	.262
1983[e]	.484	.743	.745	1.130

[a] Column 1 = Net new money for SLA divided by total national mortgage originations.

[b] Column 2 = Total deposit flows (including interest credited) dividend by total national mortgage originations.

[c] Column 3 = Net new money for SLAs relative to national savings (national income accounts concept).

[d] Column 4 = Total deposit flows relative to national savings.

[e] First half.

Source: Federal Home Loan Bank Board and Department of Commerce.

The thrift institution problem has been worsened by reduced repayments. Still, in recent years mortgage repayments have represented the major share of their total cash flow. Table 3-7 shows the ratio of SLA mortgage repayments to total mortgage originations. The distinct downtrend until 1980 was due to the fact that many borrowers had deferred prepaying their existing mortgages. New mortgage interest rates rose steadily over this period, making refinancing unattractive to homeowners, and state laws have, until late 1982, increasingly allowed the assumption of existing low-rate loans by new owners. The final column relates SLA mortgage repayments to SLA mortgage originations. Since SLA mortgage originations have been falling relative to the national level of mortgage originations, this ratio shows a less distinct trend.

DEMAND FOR MORTGAGE CREDIT[2]

Translating the expected enormous demand for housing into demand for mortgage credit involves analysis of the three major uses of mortgages: new

Table 3-7. SLA Mortgage Repayments to National and SLA Mortgage Originations.

Year	(1)[a]	(2)[b]
1970	.372	.893
1971	.349	.758
1972	.337	.695
1973	.324	.667
1974	.344	.750
1975	.359	.677
1976	.330	.601
1977	.299	.561
1978	.281	.579
1979	.266	.599
1980	.303	.664
1981	.349	.815
1982	.509	1.080
1983	.390	.659

[a] Column 1 = SLA mortgage repayments relative to national, total mortgage originations.

[b] Column 2 = SLA mortgage repayments relative to SLA mortgage originations.

Source: Federal Home Loan Bank Board and Department of Housing and Urban Development.

construction financing, resale financing when property transfers hands, and refinancing of existing houses without a sale.

The demand for mortgage credit for new houses is a function of the number of units to be financed, the price of those units, and the proportion of the value represented by the mortgage loan (the loan-to-value ratio). This analysis assumes that an average of 73 percent of the value of a new home will be financed, and that 15 percent of all new homes are paid for in cash. These values are consistent with recent historical experience.

Table 3-8 shows the demand for new home financing resulting from the three economic scenarios discussed when forecasting housing demand in Chapter 2. The base scenario postulates moderate inflation and economic growth, the optimistic scenario has higher economic growth and lower inflation, and the pessimistic has little real economic growth and higher inflation. There is over a 40 percent difference in the number of housing starts across scenarios, and new mortgage originations reflect these differences. Under the base scenario, demand for credit to finance new homes will average about $88 billion per year in the next decade. The optimistic scenario raises the demand for credit to nearly $100 billion per year; under the pessimistic scenario less than $70 billion of mortgages are originated annually.

The gross demand for resale financing can be analyzed in the same fashion. The number of resales times the average price of resale units times

Table 3-8. Demand for Mortgage Credit, 1983–1992.

	Base	Optimistic	Pessimistic
Assumption			
Growth of income	1.5%	3.0%	−0.1%
CPI inflation	8.0%	5.0%	12.0%
AAA bond rate	12.0%	10.0%	13.0%
Housing Market			
Households	1.5	1.7	1.4
Housing starts	1.7	1.9	1.3
Single-family starts	1.1	1.2	0.9
Home sales	3.2	3.5	2.6
House price inflation	6.3	6.2	6.9
Mean price (existing homes)	115,000	113,000	117,000
Mortgage Market			
New home mortgage originations	87.6	97.0	68.8
Existing home mortgage originations	215.0	236.0	159.0
Mortgage repayments (mean)	104.0	108.0	91.0
Net change in mortgage stock	199.0	225.0	137.0
Mortgage interest rate	13.0	10.8	14.2

the loan-to-value ratio will provide a gross resale origination volume. An added complication arises, however, in that most resales are accompanied by the repayment of an existing loan so that the net demand for resale financing is only about one-third of gross demand. This net demand represents households monetizing their capital gain in housing and their purchase of larger and more expensive homes. Table 3-8 shows that the gross demand for resale financing will average about $150 to $240 billion in the 1980s, with net demand averaging slightly over $100 billion. As in the case of new home financing, the pessimistic scenario lowers volume of net and gross credit demand substantially.

The final source of mortgage demand arises from the refinancing of houses by households that do not move from their present units. This explicit refinancing must be distinguished from resale financing. In most cases resale refinance is accompanied by the purchase of a large house. Explicit refinancing may be for the improvement of an existing unit, but it is more likely a result of the borrower's desire to invest in other assets or create liquidity for consumption purposes. The potential volume of refinancing is enormous given that the household's housing equity is presently estimated to be over $1.9 trillion and increasing by over $200 billion per year. Since there are no official time series data on explicit refinancing demand, and given the belief that most such credit extensions would not be directly related to housing demand, except in the sense that income from invested assets could be used for housing payments, no attempt is made here to quantify this component of mortgage credit demand.

To summarize, the net demand for mortgage credit derived from previous estimates of housing requirements will be over $2 trillion in the period from the mid-1980s to the mid-1990s. This implies a near tripling in the value of mortgages outstanding on one- to four-family properties.

THE MORTGAGE CREDIT GAP[3]

The conflicting pressure of sharply rising demand for mortgage credit and a limited supply of mortgage credit from traditional thrift institution lenders can be summarized in a concept known as the mortgage credit gap.

The procedure used measures the supply of basic mortgage credit as SLA cash flow, defined as net deposit inflow (including interest credited) plus mortgage repayments to SLAs. This cash flow is a good indicator of the funds available for acquisition of mortgages from traditional sources. Of course, mortgage originations would always be higher than this value, as other lenders would originate and hold mortgages. It is useful, however, to view secondary-market sales and purchases by other lenders and SLAs as adjustments to the "demand-supply gap," and the measurement of the gap is made without taking them into account. Thus, the gap is used merely as a hypothetical concept to illustrate the diminished role of the thrifts.

The demand for mortgage credit is determined by the number of new housing starts and existing home sales, the prices at which these transactions take place, the percentage of these properties that are financed with mortgages, and the loan-to-value ratios on the mortgaged properties. Specifically, the value of the sum of existing home sales and new housing starts is multiplied by 0.62 to derive total mortgage demand. This factor equals the proportion of properties that are mortgage financed (0.85) multiplied by the average loan-to-value ratio over the period (0.73). Actual year-to-year variations that occurred for these two factors are not considered since, again, they represent a response to the demand-supply gap.

The results of measuring the demand-supply gap in this way between 1970 and 1982 are shown in Table 3-9. The first two columns list total demand and supply of mortgage credit as just described. Column (3) represents the proportion of mortgage demand that cannot be satisfied by SLA cash flow. The resulting gap must be taken up either by variations in actual demand (due to changing mortgage terms) or by the mortgage provisions of other traditional and nontraditional holders of mortgage assets. Alternative definitions of the demand-supply gap could be derived by allowing for variations in actual demand and by including these other suppliers. A variety

Table 3-9. Measure of the Demand–Supply Gap, 1970 to 1980.

Year	Mortgage Demand ($ billions) (1)[a]	Mortgage Supply ($ billions) (2)[b]	Proportional Gap (3)[c]	Adjusted Gap (deviation from mean) (4)[d]	Current Adjusted Gap ($ billions) (5)[e]	1972 Gap ($ billions) (6)[f]
1970	35	24	0.309	0.009	0.3	0.3
1971	49	47	0.044	−0.256	−12.5	−12.9
1972	60	57	0.038	−0.262	−15.6	−15.6
1973	65	45	0.296	−0.004	−0.2	−0.2
1974	65	39	0.403	0.103	6.7	5.6
1975	76	70	0.080	−0.220	−16.7	−13.0
1976	105	87	0.168	−0.132	−13.7	−10.1
1977	141	98	0.302	0.002	0.3	0.2
1978	170	96	0.434	0.134	22.8	14.6
1979	179	88	0.506	0.206	36.8	21.2
1980	149	81	0.454	0.454	22.9	11.6
1981	130	48	0.634	0.334	43.2	22.0
1982	112	86	0.236	−0.064	−7.1	−3.0

[a] Column 1 = 0.62 × (value of sum of single-family starts and existing home sales).

[b] Column 2 = sum of mortgage repayments to SLAs and deposit flows to SLAs.

[c] Column 3 = (Column 1 minus Column 2)/Column 1.

[d] Column 4 = Column 3 − (mean of Column 3).

[e] Column 5 = Column 1 × Column 4.

[f] Column 6 = Column 5 × (consumer price index/CPI current year).

Note: These values were derived by the author.

of such calculations have been made but the general trends are very similar. The current approach has the advantage of providing a framework that can be used directly to generate projections for the 1984–92 period.

The percentage gap ranges between values near zero in 1971, 1972, and 1975 and values averaging 50 percent from 1978 to 1981. These gap values arise in part because the cash flows of other financial institutions have been excluded in carrying out the calculation. To account for this, a constant share (0.30) is subtracted to obtain the "adjusted gap" measure in the next column.[4] The last two columns provide measures of the magnitude of this adjusted gap in current and constant dollars, respectively.

The adjusted gap measure of Column (4) can be more easily interpreted. This measure corresponds well with known periods of mortgage market tightness (1970 and 1974) and ease (1971–72 and 1976). Even more interesting is the emerging trend that appears between 1978 and 1981, with a distinctly positive and large gap peaking in the crunch of 1981. This indicates a strong trend toward excess demand between 1978 and 1981, with a current dollar gap of almost $30 to $40 billion and an adjusted gap ratio of about 20 percent.

In late 1982 and in 1983 the massive inflow of funds to SLAs eliminated the gap, temporarily at least. Whether this trend is likely to continue throughout the 1980s is a matter of great concern to planners. Accordingly, projections of the adjusted gap have been made for each of the three economic scenarios portrayed in Table 3–8. Two additional assumptions that are common to the three scenarios are that the national savings rate is 5 percent annually and that SLA cash flow is 80 percent of national savings.[5]

Table 3–10 shows the annual values from 1983 to 1990 of the projected gap measures for the base scenario. The percentage gap measure declines from its value of 0.63 in 1981 to 0.14 in 1983, but then rises steadily throughout the 1980s, exceeding 55 percent in 1990. The average value of the gap over the period is 45 percent. The current dollar value of the gap rises from the 1981 value of $43 billion throughout the decade, with an average value of $41 billion. The real (1972) dollar value of the gap also rises modestly from the 1980 value of $11.6 billion, averaging $13 billion over the decade.

The projected average annual values of the three gap measures for each economic scenario were also calculated. The optimistic scenario has smaller values for each of the three gap measures than the average values of the base scenario, because the demand for mortgage funds rises more slowly than the rise in cash flow to financial institutions. This is the result of the lower house price inflation assumption that dominates the higher numbers of housing starts and existing home sales. In addition, the large deposit flows generated under the optimistic scenario lead to a greater mortgage supply and a smaller gap.

Table 3–10. Base Case Projections of the Demand–Supply Gap, 1983–1990.

Year	Mortgage Demand ($ billions) (1)[a]	Mortgage Supply ($ billions) (2)[b]	Proportional Gap (3)[c]	Adjusted Gap (deviation from mean) (4)[d]	Current Gap ($ billions) (5)[e]	Constant Dollar Gap ($ billions) (6)[f]
1983	175	150	0.143	−0.157	−27	−11.3
1984	225	118	0.475	0.175	39	15.6
1985	241	126	0.477	0.177	43	16.2
1986	246	146	0.407	0.107	26	9.2
1987	185	152	0.178	−0.122	−23	−7.7
1988	249	148	0.406	0.106	26	8.1
1989	320	145	0.546	0.246	79	23.4
1990	368	160	0.565	0.265	98	27.6

[a] Column 1 = 0.62 × (value of sum of single-family starts and existing home sales).

[b] Column 2 = 0.80 × personal savings.

[c] Column 3 = (Column 1 minus Column 2)/Column 1.

[d] Column 4 = Column 3 − (mean of Column 3).

[e] Column 5 = Column 1 × Column 4.

[f] Column 6 = Column 5 × (consumer price index/CPI current year).

Note: These values were derived by the author.

In comparison to the base case, the pessimistic scenario shows a slightly smaller percentage gap. This results from the sharply lower levels of mortgage credit demand due to the no-growth high interest rate scenario.

Overall, the results of these projection experiments for the demand-supply gap for the remainder of the 1980s are insensitive to the alternative economic scenarios, the similarities across scenarios being more striking than the differences. This insensitivity is due mainly to the fact that the chosen scenarios assume that high levels of real housing activity (starts and existing home sales) go together with relatively low rates of house price inflation, and vice versa. In contrast, a scenario, say, with both high real activity levels and high house price inflation would show a significantly larger gap. At least within the class of scenarios considered realistic, however, the projection results appear robust given the particular economic environment.

It should be emphasized that these projections represent measures of the demand-supply gap that would appear during the remainder of the 1980s *were no adjustments undertaken in the functioning and structure of the mortgage market.* In fact, important changes in the mortgage market structure will occur, significantly reducing, if not eliminating, the gap.

Market forces alone would respond to surplus demand by increasing the price of credit or the mortgage interest rate. Price is a rationing device. Higher down payments would also be expected as lenders seek to reduce risk and borrowers seek to reduce the cost of the mortgage. Both of these factors would tend to make housing at least appear to be less affordable, especially for younger households shopping for their first home. Both this mortgage credit gap and the affordability issue are at the core of movements to restructure the mortgage market.

NOTES

1. Portions of this section were taken from Dwight M. Jaffee and Kenneth T. Rosen, "The Demand for Housing and Mortgage Credit: The Mortgage Credit Gap Problem," in *Housing Finance in the Eighties: Issues and Options* (Federal National Mortgage Association, Washington, D.C., 1981).

2. This analysis of mortgage credit demand is confined to the financing of one- to four-family dwellings.

3. The material of this and the following section is an extension and revision of a discussion in Dwight M. Jaffee and Kenneth T. Rosen, "The Use of Mortgage Pass-through Securities," *New Sources of Capital for the Savings and Loan Industry* (Federal Home Loan Bank of San Francisco, 1979).

4. This is the value for the average contribution of these other institutions as calculated for the period from 1970 to 1982.

5. This is the average percentage for the period from 1972 to 1982.

Chapter 4

Cyclical Instability

Periodic cyclical declines in new housing construction result in widespread shutdowns in the building industry and curtailed activities in related industries; for example, a normal decline can produce up to a 25 percent decline in building industry production, a doubling of the construction unemployment rate, idle plant and equipment in a number of related industries, and sharp rises in the inventory of unsold homes and building-related products. This cycle is especially acute for the urban housing market. Production of new units in central cities shows far more sensitivity to tightness in monetary policy than does total housing production.

In addition to the short-run macroeconomic distress that the housing cycle creates, cyclical instability also has long-run consequences for the efficiency of the homebuilding industry. In adapting to instability the industry is forced to use a technology that may be inefficient. The industry employs a flexible, labor-intensive technology, which permits resources (workers) to be laid off during periods of slow construction activity. While efficient over a wide range of outputs, this may be inefficient at any particular output level.

The perception that the housing cycle is costly both to the industry and to society has stimulated substantial research into the nature and causes of the short cycle in housing construction. This work, most of which has been done since 1960, represents a distinct break from the previous concentration on the long cycle in housing construction.[1] The major findings correctly attribute these short-run fluctuations to the overwhelming dependency of housing on mortgage credit and to deficiencies in the housing finance system that provides this credit. In a study for the Commission on Money and Credit, Grebler and Maisel summarize their review of previous analyses with the conclusion that "while these analyses differ on matters of emphasis and detail they agree in the conclusion that short-run fluctuations in residential building have resulted mainly from changes in financial conditions labeled borrowing, availability of mortgage funds, and supply of mortgage credit."[2]

Similarly, another major study that deals in some detail with the cyclical problems of residential construction states: "The greater impact of monetary stringency on housing than on the rest of the economy apparently is due mainly to a capital rationing effect, resulting from deficiencies in current institutional arrangements for providing mortgage credit; and probably also to an interest rate effect, reflecting a greater interest elasticity of housing demand than of demand generally."[3]

The academic wisdom regarding the primary cause of fluctuations in housing construction is best summarized in a statement from a study undertaken by the Federal Reserve Board (FRB): "There is general agreement that one of the primary, if not the primary, determinants of this cyclical pattern is the similar pattern that holds with respect to a critical input in the residential construction process: the supply of mortgage credit."[4]

These mortgage availability and, to a lesser extent, mortgage cost explanations of the short-run housing cycle have had a major influence on public policy toward housing markets. Since 1968 the federal government has made attempts to moderate the fluctuations in new residential contruction. A number of governmental and quasi-governmental mechanisms have been set up in an attempt to moderate the volatility of the housing industry. The Federal National Mortgage Association (FNMA), the Federal Home Loan Bank Board (FHLBB), the Federal Home Loan Mortgage Corporation (FHLMC), and the Government National Mortgage Association (GNMA) play major roles in the effort to insulate housing from the periodic episodes of general financial restraint. These agencies appear to be acting with the knowledge and approval of the FRB to moderate the excess burden traditionally borne by the housing industry during periods of monetary stringency. These agencies are not perceived as acting contrary to macroeconomic policy; rather, they seem merely to be shifting some of the burden of this policy away from the housing industry.

An additional attempt on the part of the federal government to moderate the housing cycle was the introduction of the money market certificate (MMC) in June 1978 and the complete deregulation of deposit accounts with the introduction of the money market deposit account (MMDA) in December 1982. Another policy action aimed at moderating the present decline in housing activity was the passage of a federal override of state usury law ceilings. Finally, the extensive use of federally tax-exempt mortgage revenue bonds for single-family housing from 1979 to 1982 can also be viewed as primarily a countercyclical policy.

While the specific techniques vary, all of these agencies and policy actions work through the mortgage market to try to stabilize housing construction. Since they accept the supply credit explanation for the cycle, they all attempt to improve the flow of funds to the mortgage market. With the exception of the introduction of deregulated deposit accounts and the state usury override law, they have also attempted to reduce mortgage rates during periods of credit tightness.

HISTORIC RESIDENTIAL CONSTRUCTION CYCLES

Since World War II residential construction has experienced eight short-term cycles in activity, occurring on average every three and one-half years.[5] The average variation in activity over these cycles has been approximately 45 percent.

Table 4-1 provides a tabular analysis of the eight postwar short-term cycles in housing construction. A peak in a cycle is identified as a quarter in which the seasonally adjusted number of housing starts was greater than in the two quarters on either side of it. Likewise, a trough is identified as a quarter in which the number of housing starts was less than in the two quarters on either side.

An analysis of the data in this table indicates that the present decline in housing construction is merely a continuation of the well-known pattern of economic instability in the building industry. The housing sector has undergone major declines in 1957, 1959-60, and 1966-67, and it virtually collapsed in 1974-75 and 1980-81. New construction experienced more moderate declines in 1963-64 and 1969-70.

Each of these declines has preceded or been coincident with a recession or decline in growth in the overall economy. Conventional wisdom attributes this to the countercyclical nature of the housing industry. Residential construction is perceived as a balance wheel, tempering excess demand during periods of expansion and often leading the economywide recovery from recession. In fact, it appears that housing is at times a leading and at times a coincident indicator of overall economic activity. Due to its greater sensitivity to monetary policy changes, housing simply precedes rather than counterbalances economywide slowdowns and booms. If this view is correct, then a sharp decline in housing starts is merely a symptom of excessively stringent monetary policy that destabilizes both the housing market and, eventually, the overall economy. Rather than being countercyclical, housing is a leading indicator of instability.

This relationship between housing starts and general economic activity is demonstrated in Figure 4-1, which plots housing starts against GNPGAP —

Table 4–1.   Short-Term Cycles in New Residential Construction.[a]

Turning Points (year:quarter)	All Housing Starts (in thousands of units)[b]	Percentage Change[c]	Duration (in quarters)	Average Percentage Change (quarter to quarter)
1953:3 trough	1,235	—	—	—
1954:4 peak	1,732	+ 33.5	5	+ 6.7
1958:1 trough	1,074	− 46.9	13	− 3.6
1958:5 peak	1,647	+ 42.1	3	+ 14.0
1960:4 trough	987	− 50.1	8	− 6.3
1963:3 peak	1,676	+ 51.7	11	+ 4.7
1964:2 trough	1,489	− 11.8	3	− 3.9
1965:4 peak	1,505	+ 1.07	6	+ 0.2
1966:4 trough	919	− 48.4	4	− 12.1
1969:1 peak	1,596	+ 53.8	9	+ 6.0
1970:1 trough	1,251	− 24.2	4	− 6.1
1972:4 peak	2,451	+ 64.8	11	+ 5.9
1975:1 trough	973	− 86.3	9	− 9.6
1978:2 peak	2,127	+ 74.5	13	+ 5.7
1980:2 trough	1,064	− 66.6	8	− 8.3
1980:4 peak	1,473	+ 32.2	2	+ 16.1
1981:4 trough	853	− 26.7	4	− 6.7

	Total Magnitude	Duration	Average Percentage Change (quarter to quarter)
Average peak to trough	− 45.1	7.5	7.1
Average trough to peak	+ 44.2	6.6	7.4

[a] Excluding mobile homes.

[b] Seasonally adjusted annual rate.

[c] Adjusted for the time trend before computing percentage as:
   $100 \times$ [change in starts/((peak starts and trough starts)/2)].

Source: U.S. Bureau of the Census.

the difference between actual and potential gross national product — for the period from 1966 to 1982.[6] GNPGAP rises when the economy is in recession and falls in strong economic times. The chart shows that housing starts lead changes in GNPGAP by several quarters. The housing declines of 1966, 1969, 1974, and 1979–82 are all followed by a sharp rise in GNPGAP. Examining the housing cycle data by sector can provide additional insight into the nature of the cycle and the appropriate policy mix needed to moderate instability. (See Figure 4–2.)

The amplitude of the multifamily unit construction cycle is a little more than twice that of the single-family cycle. The sharper contractions in the

Figure 4-1. Housing Starts and GNPGAP.

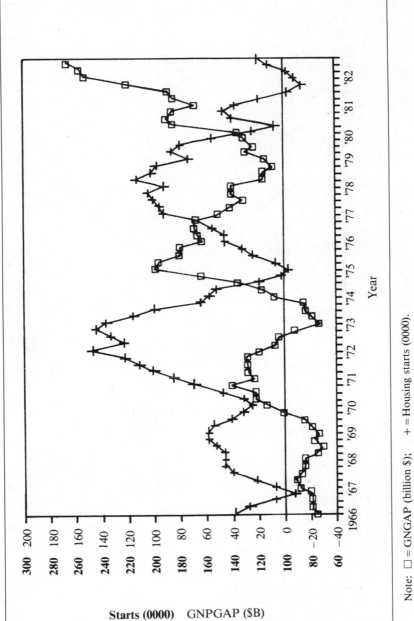

Note: □ = GNGAP (billion $);   + = Housing starts (0000).

Figure 4–2. Housing Activity; Units Started, Shipped, or Sold.

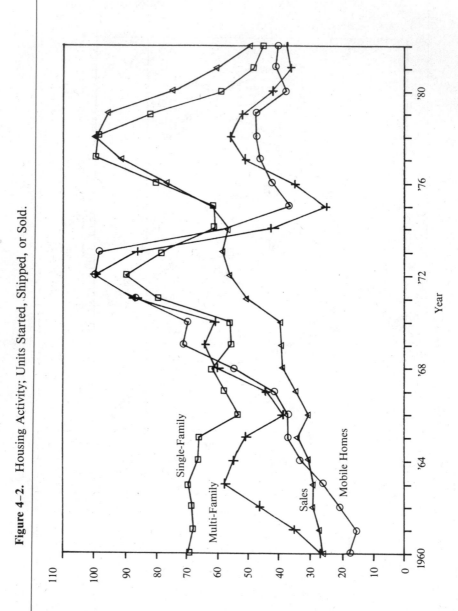

Single-Family

Multi-Family

Sales

Mobile Homes

Year as Percentage of Maximum Year

Year

multifamily sector are due to inventory accumulation, the longer production period of apartment complexes, and the greater sensitivity of investment real estate to the availability and price of mortgage credit. The 1966–67, 1974–75, and 1979–80 housing declines showed this sharper decline in the multifamily sector. However, the multifamily sector showed virtually no decline in 1970. This far greater instability in the multifamily sector implies that a policy aimed at stabilizing housing may want to focus more attention on this sector. At present virtually no federal policies directly attempt to counteract the cycle in multifamily production.

Mobile home shipments had shown far less cyclical instability until 1974–75. In 1966 and 1970 annual mobile home shipments compared to the previous year were essentially flat. In 1974–75 the upward trend in mobile home production came to an abrupt halt, with a decline in shipments paralleling the steep decline in the multifamily sector. Since that time, mobile home shipments have been at a lower but fairly stable level, showing little cyclical volatility.

A final broad measure of housing activity, existing home sales, had shown far less cyclical vulnerability than the residential construction series at least through 1979. There was a modest decline in activity in 1974, but in general the sharply rising trend in the series had offset cyclical weakness. The housing decline of the past three years indicates that the existing home sales series is showing far more vulnerability than previous history would indicate. Existing home sales dropped nearly 50 percent in the housing recession of the early 1980s. Given the important linkages between the new and resale market and the increased volatility of the resale market, the impact of countercyclical policies on this sector must be considered.

The cycle in aggregate housing production appears to be even more pronounced for inner-city markets. Table 4–2 shows the change in new housing production for a sample of central cities during two major housing declines. New central-city housing production dropped far more sharply than aggregate housing production. In 1969–70 a set of cities such as Baltimore, Chicago, Cleveland, Boston, Pittsburgh, and St. Louis showed declines in housing starts of around 50 percent. Central cities in growth areas showed a decline of 25 to 35 percent. Miami and Phoenix showed a sharp rise and small decline, respectively. At the same time, national housing starts declined only 5 percent. In 1974–75 all central cities showed dramatic declines in production, ranging from 75 to 97 percent, versus an aggregate national decline of 51 percent.

The apparent difference in cyclical sensitivity between central cities and suburban areas is caused by two factors. First, central-city housing production is primarily composed of multifamily units, which tend to exhibit a cycle twice as large as single-family production. Second, the economies of

Table 4-2. Cycle in New Production in Distressed and Nondistressed Central Cities.

	Percentage Decline 1969–1970 Peak to Trough	Percentage Decline 1975–1975 Peak to Trough
Atlanta	−26.9	−96.9
Baltimore	−59.2	−80.4
Birmingham	−35.1	−78.7
Boston	−42.2	−79.9
Chicago	−50.6	−86.5
Cleveland	−49.5	−92.7
Dallas	−32.6	−75.6
Detroit	−24.7	−84.3
Fort Lauderdale	−83.2	−94.1
Houston	−17.3	−73.4
Los Angeles	−37.0	−49.3
Miami	+62.6	−82.2
Milwaukee	−41.4	−79.7
Newark	−97.5	−60.8
New Orleans	−41.5	−82.7
New York	−21.8	−88.9
Omaha	−29.3	−76.3
Philadelphia	−10.0	−70.4
Phoenix	− 4.5	−76.4
Pittsburgh	−60.5	−90.7
St. Louis	−48.1	−97.1
San Francisco	−37.8	−72.5
San Diego	−16.7	−79.2
Tampa	−16.8	−85.8
United States	− 5.0	−50.8

Source: Raw data obtained from the U.S. Bureau of the Census, Series C-45.

central cities are more sensitive to recession-producing macroeconomic policies. This economic distress causes a corresponding decline in housing market activity.

CAUSES OF THE HOUSING CYCLE

Most of the literature on short-run fluctuations in residential construction suggests that variations in monetary policy aimed at restoring economywide stability tend to destabilize the housing sector. Recent monetary policy has attempted to control the supply of money rather than interest rates. These variations in aggregate financial restraint are first translated through the housing finance system into instability in the supply and availability of mortgage credit and then into changes in the price and other parameters of the mortgage instrument. The influence of these changes in the supply and terms of mortgage credit are then directly transmitted to the housing market.

Restrictive financial policies also have a direct effect on the housing market through their impact on the actions of the home builder. Changing financial conditions influence the builder not only through changes in expected demand but also through variation in the availability and cost of construction loans. These loans are the equivalent of working capital for nonbuilding firms. The cost of construction loans is usually tied directly to the prime rate and so is quite sensitive to variations in monetary policy.

Supply of Funds

Nearly all the studies referenced earlier correctly emphasize the primary role of the supply of mortgage credit and the secondary role of the price of credit, which results from the view that the mortgage interest rate was not an adequate indicator of the state of the mortgage markets. Unlike other markets, it was assumed that the price of the commodity (in this case mortgage credit) did not "clear the market." That is, the supply of mortgage funds did not generally equal the demand for mortgage funds at the market interest rate. This rationing or disequilibrium characteristic of the mortgage market has been responsible for the difficulty in obtaining mortgages during periods of financial restraint. During these periods nonprice rationing techniques, such as requiring very large down payments or limiting loans to large depositors of long standing, were employed.

Basic defects in the U.S. housing finance system were usually the main factors used to explain the rationing or disequilibrium phenomenon and the housing cycle. The poor portfolio balance of the major mortgage lenders, state usury ceilings on mortgage interest rates, Regulation Q ceilings on passbook accounts of thrift institutions, and Federal Housing Administration (FHA) and Veterans' Administration (VA) ceilings on mortgage interest rates were all usually cited.

The problem of cyclical instability of mortgage fund flows was centered on two portfolio choice decisions and institutional constraints under which these decisions were made. The first choice concerns the way individuals allocated their personal savings among various financial intermediaries and other assets. The second choice concerned the portfolio composition of the financial intermediaries themselves.

Individual Portfolios.   The preferences of investors concerning yield, risk, liquidity, and expected capital gains all influence their portfolio allocations between asset types. Changes in these characteristics or preferences can lead to a change in portfolio allocation.

While all of these characteristics change over the normal cycle of credit restraint and ease, variations in relative yields are of greatest importance. During periods of credit restraint the yields of financial intermediaries fell relative to open market (especially short-term) credit instruments. This was particularly true of savings and loan association (SLA) passbook accounts. As an outcome of historical precedent and government regulation, SLAs borrowed short and lent long, attracting deposits and acquiring long-term assets in the form of mortgages. In the recent past SLAs have experienced periods with negative savings flows (withdrawals in excess of deposits— disintermediation). Such liquidity crunches, often severe, resulted in drastic declines in mortgage commitments by SLAs and a sharp curtailment of housing starts.

The most likely cause of the disintermediation phenomenon experienced by financial institutions in the past decade was Regulation Q, an FRB regulation that sets the ceiling interest rates payable on commercial bank (CB) time deposit accounts. These controls have been in force since the early 1930s. Similar ceilings were applied to SLAs in 1966 by the FHLBB to prevent "cutthroat" interregional and interinstitutional competition. In 1966 SLAs were allowed to pay 0.75 percent more than CBs on passbook accounts. Over time this differential (which is also applied to certificate deposits) has fallen to 0.25 percent.

Figure 4–3 shows the relationship of SLA savings flows to the difference between the interest rate paid on six-month U.S. Treasury bills and the ceiling interest rate allowed on SLA passbook deposits; it illustrates that the disintermediation process is primarily induced by the interaction of changes of relative yields among asset types and Regulation Q ceilings.

This relationship has been examined further in a regression model relating new SLA savings flows to several variables, which confirms the strong inverse relationship illustrated in Figure 4–3. Interest rate differentials appear to have had a nonlinear effect: as ninety-one-day Treasury bill rates increased relative to SLA passbook rates, disintermediation proceeded at an accelerated rate. A similar effect emerges when three- to five-year bond rates surpass SLA rates on certificates of deposit. Finally, the model indicates that increased levels of personal savings improve the flow of funds to SLAs.

This cyclical instability of fund flows is certainly not unique to SLAs. Flows to nearly all financial intermediaries that compete for personal savings on a noncontractual basis show instability of a similar magnitude. The top portion of Table 4–3, which reports the standard deviation as a percentage of mean fund flows to six intermediaries, shows that SLAs, mutual

Figure 4–3. Flows to SLAs and Treasury Bill Ceiling Spread.

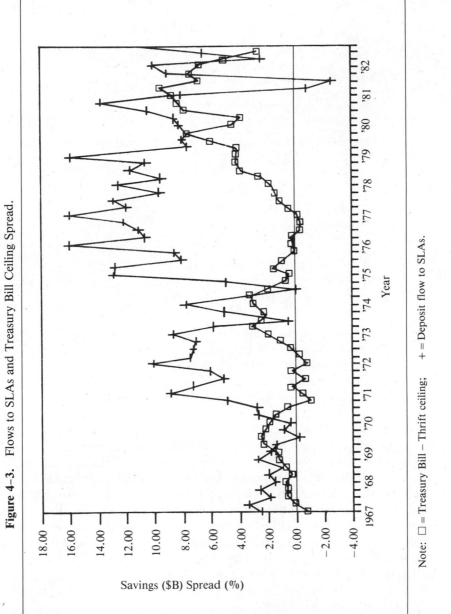

Note: □ = Treasury Bill – Thrift ceiling;   + = Deposit flow to SLAs.

Table 4-3.   Cyclical Instability of Flow to Financial Intermediaries.

	Standard Deviation as Percentage of Mean
Savings and loans	80.30
Mutual savings banks	72.98
Life insurance companies	38.32
Commercial banks — time deposits	104.59
Private pension funds	37.93
State and local retirement funds	62.12

Cyclical Instability of Mortgage Lending by Financial Intermediaries.

	Standard Deviation as Percentage of Mean
Savings and loans	55.98
Mutual savings banks	30.49
Life insurance companies	24.10
Private pension funds	76.80
State and local pension funds	68.00

Source: *Flow of Funds,* Federal Reserve Board, 1965–80.

savings banks (MSBs), and CBs experience large instability in fund flows relative to intermediaries with contractual sources of funds, such as life insurance companies (LICs) and pension funds.[7] Intermediaries that must compete with open market instruments are subject to fairly large fluctuations in fund flows caused mainly by legal restrictions and legally induced portfolio imbalances.

In turn, this cyclical instability of personal savings flows causes instability in mortgage lending. SLAs have had little choice in terms of portfolio composition. Since they are restricted primarily to the residential real estate markets, a decline in fund flows quickly leads to a decline in mortgage lending. The data presented in the lower portion of Table 4–3 show that such declines are mitigated by the ability to draw on liquid reserves, secondary-mortgage markets, FHLBB advances (loans), and the flow of repayments from presently outstanding mortgages. SLA mortgage lending is thus more stable than the flow of funds to these institutions.

Despite the mitigating effects of alternative sources of mortgage funds, there is still a strong direct relationship between housing starts and net deposit flows to SLAs. Table 4–4 indicates that prior to or coincident with each sharp decline in housing starts there was a dramatic slowdown in net deposit accumulation. In 1966 deposit flows dropped to $3.5 billion from

Table 4-4. Housing Cycles and the Supply and Price of Mortgage Credit.

Year	All Housing Starts (thousands)	Deposit Flows to SLAs ($ millions)	Mortgage Interest Rates (%)	Mortgage Rate— AAA Bond Rate (%)
1960	1,296	7,371	6.25	1.85
1961	1,365	8,423	6.02	1.67
1962	1,493	9,243	5.97	1.64
1963	1,635	10,716	5.85	1.55
1964	1,561	10,285	5.83	1.43
1965	1,510	8,159	5.87	1.38
1966	1,196	3,529	6.45	1.31
1967	1,322	10,443	6.56	1.05
1968	1,545	7,226	7.15	0.98
1969	1,500	3,853	8.02	0.99
1970	1,469	10,799	8.55	0.51
1971	2,085	26,689	7.79	0.40
1972	2,378	31,849	7.68	0.46
1973	2,057	19,860	8.32	0.89
1974	1,353	15,509	9.22	0.65
1975	1,171	41,937	9.10	0.27
1976	1,547	49,519	8.99	0.56
1977	2,002	49,987	9.01	0.99
1978	2,036	44,034	9.54	0.81
1979	1,760	38,703	10.77	1.14
1980	1,313	40,631	12.66	0.72
1981	1,100	13,302	14.70	0.53
1982	1,072	37,270	15.12	1.33

Source: U.S. Bureau of the Census, *Federal Home Loan Bank Board Journal.*

$8.2 billion the previous year, in 1969 to $3.8 billion from $7.2 billion in 1968, and in 1974 to $15.5 billion from $31.8 billion in 1972. These annual data disguise the true nature of the disintermediation process, in which net deposit flows were negative for a number of months during each cyclical decline.

In June 1978 there was a major change in the regulations on time deposit interest rate ceilings, allowing thrift institutions and CBs to issue a new certificate based on Treasury bill interest rates. The certificate had a six-month life and a minimum denomination of $10,000. The ceiling rate of the certificates was tied to the interest rate determined at the most recent six-month Treasury bill auction. This allowed the institutions to issue a deposit instrument that was competitive with open market instruments. In December 1982 further modifications of Regulation Q were made. All regulated financial intermediaries were allowed to issue MMDAs which effectively had no interest rate ceilings. It was hoped that this would enable thrift institutions to compete more effectively for savings deposits and become less susceptible to the disintermediation process, which would, in turn, reduce the instability in the availability of credit to housing and thus fluctuations in residential construction.

Institutional Portfolio Choice.   While SLAs have had until recently little portfolio flexibility because of present tax laws and regulations, other financial institutions show a moderate shift in their investments over the economic and housing cycles. These portfolio shifts generally do not work to the advantage of the housing and mortgage markets.

During periods of rising interest rates, mortgage interest rates generally fail to keep pace with rates on comparable assets. (See Table 4–4.) The spread between high-quality bonds and mortgage rates narrows in each period of tight money, exacerbating the cyclical decline in housing. Since mortgages become relatively less attractive investments, financial institutions move into other assets.

The key policy issue here is why mortgage rates are so slow to adjust to market conditions. Conventional explanations for the decline in relative mortgage interest rates during periods of credit tightness are numerous: state usury law ceilings and FHA-VA restrictions on interest rates, greater willingness on the part of business to pay higher costs for borrowed money, and the close personal relationship of borrower and lender at the typical small SLA. It is hard to document the last two reasons, but it is certain that federal interest rate ceilings on FHA-VA loans and state usury laws, intended initially to protect housing and the consumer, have become counterproductive. Of these, state usury law ceilings have been by far the more important. A "temporary" federal override of all state usury laws was enacted in March 1980 because of their negative impact on the supply of mortgage credit. This temporary override became permanent with the passage of the Gain–St. Germain legislation in October 1982.

Prohibitions and limitations on charging usury (exorbitant interest) on loans are deeply rooted in the history of civilization. These prohibitions were originally ethically or morally based and limited any type of interest payments within the community. The concept of usury gradually evolved to include only interest rates that were considered "unfair and exploitative." The prohibition of usurious interest rates was perceived as essential for the protection of naïve and unsophisticated consumers confronted by a financial market in which lenders were unethical and had superior market power. Proponents of usury law contended that it was necessary to legislate "fair" interest rates in this situation. The populist justification was also often evoked: usury ceilings were viewed as a tool for income redistribution from the wealthy to the poor by reducing the "unearned income" of lenders.

Despite their apparently benign origins, these ceilings became a major source of inefficiency in mortgage markets in the late 1970s to the detriment of wealthy and poor alike. The sharp rise in inflation in the economy induced a substantial rise in nominal interest rates. Usury ceilings, which in previous years had been at levels nearly twice the interest rate on normal market transactions, at times became binding constraints on market transactions in nearly twenty states. In addition, the state usury ceilings may have had a negative impact on the very people they were meant to protect: by constraining the yield on loans they encouraged credit rationing and discrimination against risky (i.e., poor and disadvantaged) borrowers. If the appropriate risk premium cannot be changed, loans may become unavailable or be available only with restrictive noninterest rate terms.

Mortgage Demand

In addition to the direct influence of the supply of mortgage credit on housing activity, changes in the terms that characterize the mortgage instrument also have substantial effects on the demand for residential construction. The mortgage instrument has three major components—the contract interest rate; the amount of the loan, which in combination with the price of the house determines the down payment requirement; and the amortization period of the loan—which are simultaneously determined.[8]

Variations in mortgage interest rates traditionally have been considered one of the prime determinants of new housing activity. There seems to be complete agreement that, in the short run, increases in mortgage interest rates reduce the demand for mortgages and the number of housing starts. There are several channels through which mortgage interest rates affect the demand for housing starts.

An increase in the real mortgage rate—the nominal rate (market rate) minus the expected inflation rate—would be expected to have a negative impact on activity. Even if the real mortgage rate is unchanged, a higher expected inflation rate raises the nominal rate and increases monthly mortgage payments immediately. This would also be expected to reduce the demand for starts since more borrowers would be led to postpone purchases and more would be disqualified under current cost-current income lending criteria.

The net impact of these demand effects is substantial. Econometric estimates of the short-run elasticity of housing starts to changes in the mortgage interest rate average around -1.5. This implies that a 10 percent increase in mortgage rates will cause a 15 percent decline in housing starts.[9]

Down payment requirements also considerably influence short-run fluc-tuations in housing. Lower down payments stimulate demand and housing starts by reducing the need for households to generate large front-end pay-ments. Most research has shown a strong inverse relationship between changes in down payment requirements and housing starts. The short-run elasticity of housing starts, with respect to the down payment, is estimated at around -2.3: a 10 percent decrease in down payment requirements will stimulate a 23 percent increase in housing starts. This large elasticity is caused in part by the fact that the down payment requirement is the mech-anism many lenders use to ration credit during periods of financial restraint.

The amortization period of the mortgage loan would be expected to have a direct relationship to housing activity. Longer amortization periods lead to lower monthly payments even though they increase the total payments by the household (principal and interest) over the life of the loan. There is little econometric evidence on the short-run impact of changing amortization periods on housing starts. It is theoretically clear that longer amortization periods should increase the demand for housing.

COSTS OF CYCLICAL INSTABILITY

Measuring the costs of cyclical instability in housing construction is an extremely difficult task. First, the effects are not confined to the housing industry; they are also felt by the full set of firms whose demand is wholly or partially derived from housing construction. Second, if new home produc-tion had the same instability as the average industry in the United States, other sectors of the economy might have to experience greater economic in-stability than is presently the case. In a total measure of the cost of insta-bility in housing production to society, this tradeoff between sectors should be taken into account. This is clearly beyond the scope of this book, and the following analysis looks only at the housing sector.

In assessing the costs of instability on housing construction, two effects can be isolated. The first effect concerns where along the existing industry cost curve the industry produces its output. The weighted average of pro-duction levels times cost increases will then provide a direct measure of the cost of an unstable pattern of production versus a stable pattern of home production. The second effect concerns the slope of the cost curve itself. This effect is not easily quantified, as it involves a "what if" experiment. Theoretically, instability of demand should prompt the profit-maximizing firm to trade off static efficiency for the advantages of flexibility. The firm will choose a production technology that will be able to handle a wide band of outputs but will not be efficient at any single output. Thus, the cost of production in an unstable environment will be higher than in a more stable environment. In essence, the slope and intercept of the cost curve will have shifted in an unstable environment. Given the complexity involved in measuring the cost of instability, only the "movement along the cost curve" impact was quantified, and the estimate given should be viewed as a lower bound of the cost of instability to the industry.

An equation was estimated, by the author, relating the cost of construction, as measured by the Department of Commerce Composite Construction Cost Index, to the level of residential and nonresidential construction. [10] This equation shows that construction costs are highly sensitive to changes in the level of construction output, with the elasticity of construction costs with respect to housing starts substantially over two. This high elasticity arises because of the capacity constraints and bottlenecks the industry quickly encounters as it approaches the level of 2 million starts per year. A more stable environment would first allow the average cost of housing production over the economic cycle to be lower. The nonlinear nature of the cost curve ensures that cyclical instability will increase the weighted average cost of production as increasing costs at higher output levels are experienced. Second, in a more stable environment the coefficients of the cost curve might themselves be lower. A simulation experiment with this curve indicates that over a ten-year period housing costs would be as much as 5.3 percent higher than in a more stable environment.

SUMMARY

Cyclical fluctuations in the housing market have significant economywide ramifications. The cause of this cyclical instability problem is the sensitivity of housing construction to financial restraint due to the great dependency of purchasers on credit and to deficiencies in the housing finance system. Credit influences the housing market directly through the availability of loans to builders and consumers. Thus, construction activity is both directly and indirectly influenced through changes in mortgage terms.

The costs of cyclical instability are numerous. Short-run construction declines lead to a doubling of the construction unemployment rate, idle plant and capital equipment in related industries, and sharp rises in the inventory of unsold homes and building-related products. Cyclical instability also has many long-run consequences. The efficiency of the homebuilding industry is affected by the use of a flexible, labor-intensive technology that, while suitable for a wide range of outputs, can be inefficient at a particular output level. Periodic fluctuations in homebuilding also can lead to substantial start-up and shutdown costs, often involving bankruptcy. The ensuing inventory during periods of inactivity is reflected in increased holding costs throughout the housing production system.

Quantifying these costs is difficult, but econometric analysis indicates that cyclical instability in the housing market relative to the cycle of the overall economy does increase the cost of housing production. This cost of instability is substantial enough to warrant the attention of policymakers.

Public policy toward the cyclical instability in mortgage lending causes fluctuations in housing activity. As a result, stabilizing the flow of mortgage credit to the housing market appears to have become a major goal of federal housing policy since the mid-1960s. The establishment of the FHLMC, the reorganization of the FNMA, the new aggressiveness of the FHLBB, and the reorientation of the GNMA can all be viewed as attempts to insulate mortgage and housing markets from general financial restraint. The activities of these agencies have also led to an increased federalization of the private housing finance system.

In addition to the role of these agencies, since mid-1978 public policy toward cyclical instability has taken a surprising new turn. Following the long-standing recommendations of housing economists, the deregulation of the housing finance system has finally taken place. Starting with the introduction of the MMC and culminating with the introduction of the unregulated MMDA in December 1982, the inflexibility of Regulation Q ceilings has been virtually eliminated. The passage of the federal override of state usury law ceilings and the complete deregulation of the asset structure of SLAs should provide these institutions with the flexibility to meet the volatile environment of the mid- and late 1980s. As a result of these actions, federal policy appears to be directly confronting the cause of the cyclical instability problem.

NOTES

1. Long cycles of fifteen to twenty-five years are attributed to wars, income, immigration, and household formations. See Leo Grebler, David Blank, and Louis Winnick, *Capital Formation in Residential Real Estate,* National Bureau of Economic Research (Princeton, N.J.: Princeton University Press, 1956).

2. Leo Grebler and Sherman Maisel, "Determinants of Residential Construction: A Review of Present Knowledge," *Impacts of Monetary Policy, Commission on Money and Credit* (Englewood Cliffs, N.J.: Prentice Hall, 1963).

3. Quote by Irwin Friend, "Summary and Recommendations," in *Study on the Savings and Loan Industry,* vol. 1 (Washington, D.C.: Government Printing Office, 1970), p. 8. Federal Home Loan Bank Board. "'Elasticity' measures the proportional response of one variable to changes in another. A high interest elasticity of housing demand indicates that mortgage interest rate changes generate greater than proportional changes in housing demand."

4. James B. Burnham, "Private Financial Institutions and the Residential Mortgage Cycle, with Particular Reference to the Savings and Loan Industry," in FRB,

Board of Governors, *Ways to Moderate Fluctuation in Housing Construction* (Washington, D.C.: Government Printing Office, 1972), p. 81.

5. Short-term cycle refers to those variations (exclusive of seasonal factors) that occur around long-term trends.

6. Potential GNP is calculated assuming an economy at "full employment," presently estimated to have been achieved with a 6 percent unemployment rate. If the unemployment rate were below 6 percent, GNPGAP could be negative.

7. The standard deviation is a popular measure of the dispersion or variability of a sample of data. Dividing this statistic by the mean or average value of that sample makes one set of observations more directly comparable with another. In the present application this measure is flawed because it ignores time trends in the values of these means.

8. For a more extended analysis see J. Kearl, K. Rosen, and C. Swan, *Relationships between the Mortgage Instrument, the Demand for Housing and Mortgage Credit: A Review of Empirical Studies,* Federal Reserve Bank of Boston (MIT–HUD Alternative Mortgage Study, September 1975).

9. Ibid.

10. The equation shows that the construction industry, including material supplies and on-site labor input, faces the usual nonlinear U-shaped cost curve. See C. Manski and K. Rosen (1978) for a more extensive treatment of the cost of cyclical instability. "The Implications of Demand Instability for the Behavior of Firms: The Case of Residential Construction," *Journal of Urban and Real Estate Economics* (August 1978).

Change in "Real" Construction Costs =

$$165.6 + 1.61 \text{ (Volume of nonresidential construction put in place)}$$
$$(3.8) \quad (2.0)$$

$$+ 2.35 \text{ (Housing starts, lagged one year)}$$
$$(2.2)$$

Period: 1964–78 $R^2 = .55$ D.W. $= 1.96$ t statistics in ( ).

Chapter 5

Land-Use and Rent Control Regulations

Local policy responses to housing market problems primarily have been directed at two areas: land-use regulations and rent control. Although these local policies may seem appropriate in the short run, they do not solve the basic problems. Because they tend to inhibit housing production, reducing the ability to meet the demand for housing, in the long run they may be detrimental.

Local land-use controls take a number of forms: zoning, growth management systems, subdivision regulations, and environmental restrictions are the most common. But, while they seem sound environmentally and while they serve many political purposes, these regulations put constraints on the housing market that are a direct cause of housing problems, leading to shortages and increased housing prices.

Rent control, which has been initiated at the local level in reaction to housing shortages and rapidly rising prices in the rental market, often appear, from the local perspective, to be a reasonable response. This view is shortsighted. In the long run, rent control actually intensifies rental housing problems.

LAND-USE CONTROLS

Traditionally, proponents of land-use controls have claimed that they were working to promote the health, safety, and general welfare of the residents of a community. During the late 1960s and early 1970s many communities became increasingly dissatisfied with the effects of unrestrained growth and undirected development on the natural environment. The result was a proliferation of land-use regulations. Although restrictions were enacted at all levels of government, the bulk of these controls stem from local policy decisions. The result of this increase in controls is that the homebuilding industry must now work within a much more complex and costly regulatory framework.

Local governments use numerous mechanisms to control the location, timing, character, and amount of residential development. Traditionally, communities have relied upon zoning and subdivision ordinances, building codes, and communitywide land-use plans as the major tools for the regulation of new development. Since the mid-1970s more sophisticated and complex regulatory procedures have been developed and widely applied at the municipal level. These include environmental and fiscal impact analyses, urban growth management systems, utility connection moratoriums, multiple permit systems, and limits on overall growth.

These provisions affect almost every component of housing costs. Regulations that restrict the supply of developable land or restrain density by, for example, imposing a minimum lot size can greatly increase raw land costs. Regulations on improvements, the provision of amenities, and subdivision design can add significant costs to lot preparation. The costs of structural material and labor can be increased by building codes and other regulations that designate minimum house size or require other major design changes. Substantial carrying costs can be imposed by administrative delays.

Zoning and Growth Management Systems

Zoning allocates parcels of land to particular uses. Historically, its primary purpose has been to separate "incompatible" land uses, thereby mitigating the negative spillover effects associated with certain types of land use. Zoning to prevent these negative neighborhood effects can be called "externality zoning," since it operates to reduce the negative impact of externalities that would occur in an unregulated market. Highly restrictive zoning has also been justified on the grounds that it protects or enhances property values, preserves a "rural atmosphere," and ensures the community against fiscally burdensome development, whereby new residents of an area impose more public costs than they pay in taxes.

This technique often works to maintain homogeneity within a community, excluding groups considered undesirable by current residents. In particular, fiscal zoning usually means the exclusion of multifamily dwelling units and low- or middle-income households. Critics assert that zoning is merely a mechanism for achieving segregation by maintaining housing costs at a level high enough to exclude anyone with an income lower than that earned by existing residents. It is interesting to note that in many cases current residents could not afford to buy the homes they live in, given present prices and interest rates.

Zoning ordinances can influence housing costs in several ways, but their most important effect is probably on raw (unimproved) land costs. Restricting the supply of developable land increases land prices, and minimum lot size regulations often increase the land cost per dwelling unit. Moreover, architectural standards and minimum floor area requirements often included in zoning ordinances may work to increase administrative, land development, and actual construction costs.

The effect of zoning on raw land costs depends on the extent to which it actually modifies the allocation of land to alternative uses. If zoning does induce significant changes in the amount of land allocated to various uses, then the prices of land in overallocated categories will be depressed relative to prices in an unzoned market, and prices in the underallocated categories will be elevated relative to those in an unzoned market.

The effects of zoning and land use on the supply and price of land can be illustrated by the following simple analytical model. (For a graphic presentation of the material, see Appendix 5A.) In the unzoned competitive market, equilibrium occurs when total demand for land by each group of users equals the total land supply available to each group. At this point the price of land in each of the submarkets is the same; housing developers would consume a portion of the land, other users would utilize the remainder of the supply, and the supply and demand interaction would determine price and land allocation.

In a situation in which zoning ordinances limit the supply of land for housing purposes, however, there is less land available for housing and more land available for other uses. If the supply allocated for housing is greater than the demand for housing, land-use restrictions would not have any effect on the price of housing. But, on the other hand, if the supply allocated for housing is less than the effective demand for housing, zoning would create two separate submarkets for land. In this case the restriction on the supply of land would increase the price of the land used for housing while increasing the supply and reducing the price of land for other uses.

The price elasticity of demand for residential land is the major element determining the price effect of a restriction on the supply of residential land. The more inelastic the demand, the larger the price increase. Overall, the effect of a supply restriction on the price of land for residential development depends on the amount of land removed, the permanence of the restriction, and the price elasticity of demand, which is related to the opportunity for escaping the restrictions by developing substitute housing elsewhere. This is exactly the type of zoning that communities concerned with maintaining environmental quality or fiscal balance use to limit the supply of residential land.

Translating these zoning effects on the cost of land into the housing market is straightforward. The increased cost of land implies an upward shift of the supply curve of new housing. It also implies that the supply curve of new housing rises more steeply, as there is a need to get costly variances and rezoning to develop in certain areas. For any given set of zoning regulations, however, the effect on house prices will depend on the price elasticity of demand for new housing. The more elastic the demand, the less the price increase. Since in a controlled region it is often difficult to obtain variances or construction permits to have land rezoned, the cost of land, and therefore the cost of housing, rises dramatically. This is exactly the situation that occurred after the recession in 1974–75: land prices spurted because it took a long time to get needed approvals, yet housing demand recovered quickly. When demand shows wide fluctuations in a restrictive land-use environment, housing becomes far more costly.

In addition to reducing the supply of developable land, zoning can also raise costs by restricting intensity of development. Large-lot zoning directly raises the price of land per unit and also indirectly raises house prices by leading to larger floor areas and house sizes. (Figure 5A–2 can also be employed to analyze this situation by simply considering that the horizontal axis measures potential number of units, reduced because of the larger acreage requirement per unit.)

This same analytic framework is also applicable to growth management systems, which can be viewed as "dynamic" or "conditional" zoning plans. Rather than fixing the specific amounts of land dedicated to particular uses (as in Figure 5A–1) growth management systems typically make these restrictions contingent on other factors such as time (growth rate ceilings) or the availability of adequate public support facilities. In this way the burden growth places on municipal treasuries and infrastructures is moderated. Again, the cost of these controls is manifested in higher home prices in the affected and surrounding regions.

In San Jose, California, an adequate public facilities ordinance was passed in 1973 to alleviate overcrowding in schools by controlling residential development. This ordinance made the availability of school space a condition for approval to develop and placed a moratorium on residential building permits in certain areas unless they were approved by the local school board and city council. This provision augmented the city's urban development policy established in 1970. This policy partitioned San Jose into an urban service area (where most development was concentrated), an urban transition area, and an urban reserve (essentially removed from the developable land supply). Several studies concluded that between 1967 and 1976 at least 20 to 30 percent of housing cost increases in this area could be directly attributed to local growth management policies.

Other communities have attempted to control growth through growth management timing ordinances or annual building permit limitations or both. In Ramapo, New York, the growth management system is based on phased development controls that link development permits to the availability of certain public facilities while directly controlling the location and the timing of the latter. In Petaluma, California, the growth management system combines ceilings on the annual number of units that can be built by both type and location with various requirements relating to the availability of services, the quality of design, and the environmental and fiscal impact on the community.

Although the ostensible goal of a growth control system is to reduce the fiscal, social, and environmental costs of growth to a community, these costs do not easily disappear. Often, the result is simply a shifting of costs to other communities, developers, and prospective homebuyers and renters. Overall, growth management systems have a potentially significant inflationary effect on housing prices. They tend to increase land costs by restricting development to serviced areas. Through the competition for development approval, residential allocation systems encourage developers to provide high-cost amenities that greatly increase land development costs and often force developers to reorient projects to a higher income market. In addition, growth management programs are usually complex and often impose substantial administrative costs.

Subdivision Regulations

Early subdivision ordinances required only the disclosure of certain engineering and surveying information as a prerequisite for plot approval. Present-day ordinances, however, often demand numerous on-site and off-site improvements and involve complex and often lengthy approval procedures. Sewers, streets, drainage and water lines, curbs, shade trees, and many other public improvements that, fifty years ago, were typically provided or built by the municipal government and financed by special assessments against property owners in the immediate neighborhood have today almost universally become the responsibility of the residential developer.

The standards for subdivision design and the number of required improvements have increased drastically over the years. Although these regulations have generally improved residential environments, they have also increased lot preparation costs. Subdivision regulations increase housing costs through increased improvement requirements; the shifting of public service costs to the developer; delays; and the increased administrative, planning, and engineering costs of various fiscal and environmental impact assessments.

The extreme difficulty of determining whether a minimum standard or requirement is necessary or excessive is the fundamental problem in analyzing land-use controls. Many controls are necessary or desirable in providing amenities and preserving the quality of the living environment. As such, they are quite properly reflected in higher house costs. However, it is generally believed that subdivision ordinances frequently impose standards for improvements that add costs beyond those needed for the protection of public health and safety.

Subdivision regulations can also increase housing costs by shifting the public service costs of new development from the municipality to developers themselves. Communities that have traditionally covered the bulk of public service costs of new residential development have become increasingly conscious of the fiscal impact of land development. In places such as California, where taxing limitations were passed by statewide initiative (Propositions 13 and 4), this fiscal awareness is acute.

The major instrument utilized by communities to shift public facilities costs to developers has been the imposition of substantial fees and taxes as well as land dedication (donation for specific public use) requirements on new developments. The costs of public facilities and of processing the development is passed on to the developer through school impact fees, sewer and water connection or facilities fees, capital improvements fees, park fees, storm drainage fees, construction taxes, subdivision map filing fees, and miscellaneous other charges. In the San Francisco Bay area, development fees on a three-bedroom house are as high as $8,500 in some communities, and the regional mean fee level was over $3,000 for a standard three-bedroom home in the summer of 1981, with more fee increases expected under the continuing impact of Proposition 13.

Although many fees reflect the actual costs of providing services to the new development, there are numerous examples where the revenues generated by the change not only cover the costs of services to the new development but also provide services for the general community. In this case development charges act as exclusionary instruments, raising the costs of housing and extracting inequitable surcharges from new residents for the benefit of existing property owners.

Subdivision requirements can add substantial administrative costs. The carrying costs imposed by delay consist of the interest costs of land development financing, the opportunity costs of the capital tied up in the project, the additional property tax on the land, staff wages, and other increased overhead costs. The uncertainty and risk involved in the regulatory process may also increase the developer's required profit margin. Homebuilders estimate that each additional month added to the completion date of a unit can increase the final selling price by up to 2 percent. A national survey of builders about the length of time necessary to gain development approval found that in 1970, 72.2 percent of the developers interviewed obtained approval to develop in less than seven months; only 2.8 percent required over a year to gain approval. By 1975 only 14.5 percent were able to gain permission in less than seven months, and 58 percent needed over a year.[1] It is generally perceived that this delay in gaining approval for development continues to be a major problem for developers today.

Environmental Regulations

The tremendous increase in environmental consciousness in the late 1960s fostered a commitment to protect the physical environment from the damaging aspects of unrestrained suburban growth. Environmentalists characterize suburbia as inefficient and ugly, and they attack sprawling developments as unnecessarily adding to public service and improvement costs and damaging the natural environment. Environmental regulations and many growth management techniques assert that their primary objectives are providing for the more compact use of land and channeling developments into areas where they will not damage important features of the natural environment. While often serving such desirable purposes, these regulations also increase housing costs and limit the provision of middle-income housing. Moreover, in many areas environmental groups increasingly have shown hostility to growth of any kind, including development that is environmentally sound.

Environmental regulations take the form of plans for the preservation of open space and regulations governing the management of coastal land, and they are often an important element of growth management programs. The most prominent of them is the environmental impact review (EIR). EIR procedures aim to assemble accurate measures of the major effects of new development on municipalities and regions and to apply this information to the land-use planning process. The analysis of the environmental impacts of development are contained in an environmental impact statement (EIS); preparation of this statement is usually the responsibility of the developer, who typically engages consultants to do the actual analysis and forecasting.

EIRs add to housing costs in several ways. They impose the direct costs of preparing the EIR and the costs of the public review. By the time a development reaches the formal EIR stage, the developer typically has already bought the land and invested in various planning studies. This means that delays caused by the EIR process can impose significant carrying costs. Regulations resulting from the EIR process might also increase the cost of housing by mandating expensive alterations in the physical characteristics of new residential developments to make them comply with EIR requirements.

Evidence suggests that EIR procedures do provide important benefits by reducing some of the adverse effects of unconstrained development. In many instances EIRs have proved successful in altering development so as to prevent increased traffic congestion or the degradation of important wild-life habitats. Although the EIR process can produce significant improvements, the benefits go mainly to existing residents and the costs fall primarily on developers and buyers of new homes. Higher housing costs and diminished housing availability are felt most by moderate- and low-income groups. The changes in development plans often required for EIR compliance usually lead to fewer units being built and to the reorientation of the existing units to a higher income group.

LAND-USE CONTROLS AND HOUSING COSTS: THE CALIFORNIA EXPERIENCE

It is well known that California house prices are the highest in the country, exceeding the national median by over 60 percent. What is not well known, however, is that less than ten years ago California house prices were at the national median. This dramatic surge in house prices in California has coincided with three other phenomena: a large increase in net migration to California from the rest of the country, a surge in household formations as a result of the maturation of the post–World War II baby boom generation, and a massive increase in the use of land-use and growth management techniques to slow and stop new housing production. Although there is a direct causal relationship between all of these phenomena and the sharp acceleration in California house prices, the most important by far is the stringent land-use regulations imposed in the 1970s.

Table 5–1 shows the large differences in land costs between California and a representative sample of other parts of the country in 1979. Land costs per square foot were nearly twice as high in California as anywhere else in the country and triple those in states with average land costs, such as Texas. An average tiny California lot costs nearly $30,000 – over $140,000 per acre. This compares with a $10,000 to $12,000 lot ($45,000 per acre) elsewhere in the country. A response to this high cost of land is that California lots are typically less than 0.2 acres, about one-third less than the U.S. average. Even with this smaller lot size, land costs constitute 27 percent of the value of new homes in California versus 18.7 percent nationally. As Table 5–1 also reveals, this high cost of developed lots in California is not mirrored by a high price for undeveloped farm land. California farm land values are only a little above average and far below values in places such as Illinois and New Jersey. Nor is it caused by such factors as population density, higher income, or more compact urban areas, as many eastern states surpass California in these statistics. The main explanation for the higher costs for developed lots seems to rest with local land-use regulations.

Table 5-1. 1979 Land Costs in Selected States.[a]

	Average Cost of Lot	Average Cost of Lot per Square Foot ($)	Average Cost of Lot per Acre ($)	Average Size of Lot (acres)	Average Cost of Farm Land per Acre ($)	Average Sale Price of House ($)
California	28,466	2.96	142,906	0.199	844	103,698
Colorado	12,613	1.44	69,750	0.181	297	71,034
Florida	12,049	1.13	54,477	0.220	838	58,277
Georgia	9,839	0.52	25,281	0.389	491	60,220
Illinois	16,484	1.57	76,029	0.217	1,484	83,270
Michigan	12,986	0.95	46,146	0.281	708	69,363
Mississippi	9,174	0.70	34,069	0.269	424	56,447
Missouri	10,427	0.89	43,065	0.242	560	68,756
New Jersey	16,486	0.98	47,204	0.341	1,884	71,019
Texas	9,689	0.96	46,245	0.209	320	63,474
Virginia	15,754	1.19	57,778	0.272	672	74,627

[a] This sample represents the largest and most active states in terms of new housing construction.

Source: Derived from Proprietary Builder Survey and Department of Agriculture, *Farm Real Estate*.

Table 5-2.   Land Costs and Housing Costs, 1976 and 1979.

	Average Cost of Lot in Dollars per Square Foot			Average Cost of House in Dollars per Square Foot		
	1976	*1979*	*Percentage Change*	*1976*	*1979*	*Percentage Change*
California	1.57	2.96	88.5	36.01	54.81	52.2
Colorado	.95	1.44	51.5	27.43	41.88	52.7
Florida	.95	1.13	18.9	28.85	34.85	20.8
Georgia	.45	.52	15.6	31.99	34.35	7.4
Illinois	1.09	1.57	44.0	34.04	48.52	42.6
Michigan	.72	.95	31.9	30.93	40.05	29.5
Missouri	.79	.89	12.7	29.01	37.82	30.4
New Jersey	.79	.98	24.1	31.27	36.87	17.9
Texas	.69	.96	39.1	24.34	36.54	50.1
Virginia	.87	1.19	36.8	31.95	42.26	32.2

Source: Derived from Proprietary Builder Survey.

Further confirmation of this view is provided in Table 5-2, which shows land and housing prices in 1976 and 1979 and the percentage change over this period. The increase in land costs in California is nearly double that of these other states for this period, which was marked by an increase in the prevalence of land-use controls in California.

In order to test this proposition more rigorously, an econometric model of the determinants of the cost of housing in the San Francisco metropolitan area has been developed. Data on home sales for sixty-four communities for the period from January to June 1979 were obtained from the Society of Real Estate Appraisers Data Base. These data provided information on sale price, size, age, and condition of houses that were sold in the sample time period. Community averages were computed from the raw individual transaction data for each of the housing data series. Data on other variables such as income, journey to work, property taxes, and local public expenditures, were obtained from various state and county agencies.[2]

Finally, data on growth controls and the fees associated with growth management were obtained from two extensive land-use policy surveys of local officials done in 1979. Most of the data on specific growth management policies were derived from a mail and telephone survey by the Center for Real Estate and Urban Economics (CREUE) at the University of California, Berkeley. Data on fees and charges were obtained from a survey of development fees by the Association of Bay Area Governments (ABAG).

The basic model is a simple hedonic house price equation. Prices in community X are specified as a function of house characteristics (size and age), community characteristics (average income, property tax rates, and commute time to downtown San Francisco), and land-use variables. Since the land-use variables were constructed from our surveys, they need further explanation.

The major land-use variable concerns the presence of a growth moratorium or a growth management plan in the community, affecting all new residential single-family development. If the community had such a plan in effect prior to 1976, it was assigned a value of 1. If there was a shorter moratorium or a recently instituted growth plan, the community was assigned a value of 0.25 to 0.75, depending on answers to other survey questions that indicated the degree of antigrowth sentiment in the locality. Communities that had no moratorium or growth management plan were assigned a value of 0. This variable probably leads to underestimates of the total significance of a growth control program, since it does not account for spillover effects into nearby communities.

The second land-use variable is merely the average development fees per unit required for a small single-family home development in the community. It combines the CREUE and ABAG development fee surveys. The results indicate that this specification explains variations in house prices across jurisdictions in the San Francisco Bay area quite well. With the exception of the journey to work, all the explanatory variables are highly significant.

Larger houses and older homes command higher prices. Houses in higher income and lower property tax communities also command higher prices. Finally, the measure of land-use stringency has a strong positive impact on house prices. Many different versions of the basic model confirm these results and attribute an 18 to 28 percent increase in housing costs to these land-use regulations. The full econometric results are shown in Appendix 5A.

These results are not surprising given the widespread use of controls in San Francisco Bay area communities, which limits the available supply response in neighboring communities. If these techniques spread to non-California metropolitan areas, they clearly will have negative consequences on the affordability of housing for the maturing post–World War II baby boom cohort now entering the housing market.

RENT CONTROL

The Rental Housing Problem

Rent control became a popular form of local regulation as a result of housing shortages in many rapidly growing older urban metropolitan areas, generally low vacancy rates, and a perception on the part of consumers and politicians that rents were rising very rapidly. In fact, rents in the 1970s have failed, by a wide margin, to keep pace with general price rises.

Many analysts believe that the rental housing problem actually centers on the problem of inadequate rents, which have not risen enough to cover increased construction and operating costs while still providing a return to investors in rental housing comparable to that available elsewhere in the economy. However, since rental costs constitute a high percentage of low and lower-middle income budgets, even modest rent increases appear large relative to increases in income and thus evoke considerable opposition. Unable to "vote with their feet" because of low vacancy rates, renters have increasingly turned to the political system for rent control regulations.

The increased interest in rent control has been spurred by recent trends in the rental housing market. Between 1965 and 1974 rental vacancy rates experienced a drastic decline. Not even the construction boom of the early 1970s could greatly alter this trend. Since 1974 vacancy rates have continued to decline in many areas, especially those with operational or contemplated rent control programs. In such metropolitan areas as Los Angeles, San Francisco, and San Diego the rental vacancy rate has fallen well below the 5 percent rate typically considered the minimum necessary in a normally functioning housing market.

Despite tight markets, private supply response has been slow. This has been attributed to divergent trends in income, prices, and costs in rental markets since the mid-1960s. These trends have created a situation in which rental housing is simultaneously less profitable to investors and less affordable to renters.

On the cost side the median gross rent has risen 54.6 percent since 1970 on a national basis. This compares with a rise in renter median income of only 28.6 percent over the same period. At the same time, the overall inflation rate in the economy rose 60 percent and construction costs rose over 70 percent. These highly divergent trends in costs, prices, and incomes in the past decade have created a rental price-income squeeze for tenants and construction cost-rental price squeeze for builders. In order to increase new production, the rental price would have to rise even faster than the income of tenants. These divergent trends have created a major dilemma for policymakers. They also explain such phenomena as the spread of rent control in the face of relatively slowly rising rents. While a good explanation has never been offered for these trends, it is apparent that the income of tenants, because of an increasing concentration of low-income households in rental units, would not support the rent increases necessary to meet new construction costs. Thus, the extremely tight rental supply in many areas of the country due to the lack of new construction is not likely to be resolved without a dramatic increase in tenant income. Low-income tenants on relatively fixed incomes are seeing their rent-income ratios rise and also experiencing the decreased purchasing power of the remainder of their income.

This trend is partially due to the self-selection process. Former tenants who increasingly have opted to purchase their own homes have been at the higher end of the renter income distribution. Therefore, the remaining population in rental units exhibits a higher proportion of lower income households: the percentage of households paying over 35 percent of their income for rent rose from 23 percent in 1970 to 34 percent in 1980. These facts substantiate the possibility of a growing housing affordability problem for renters, even though rents are not rising as fast as the prices of other goods.

Landlords and developers see this situation in quite a different light, whereby the cost of constructing and operating a unit has risen relative to rental income, making it unprofitable to build nonsubsidized rental housing units. This trend has created a cost-price gap of over 30 percent in many parts of the country. Cash flow is frequently negative, and even with appreciation in property values, rental housing is a difficult investment to justify in comparison to other investment alternatives. Rents would have to rise from 25 to 40 percent in most parts of the country to make a new rental housing project economically acceptable.

The supply problem has been exacerbated by the trend toward converting rental units into owner-occupied condominium or cooperative units. Landlords facing a rental rate of return far below market levels find that they can achieve a higher return by liquidating rental real estate investment. The high demand for these homeowner units is a clear incentive for landlords. Although this depletes the rental housing stock it also has the benefit of adding to the lower-cost, owner-occupied housing stock, thereby allowing more young and lower income households to become first-time homebuyers. However, the rental housing shortage is approaching critical dimensions in many parts of the country. Nationally, the vacancy rate is near its lowest point in twenty years. This renders mobility difficult. Renters tend to remain stationary, and those who are forced to move are likely to encounter rent increases and a tightening housing market.

Under these circumstances rent control seems attractive to renters and politicians, but it does not attack the real problem: a shortage of affordable housing. Ultimately, this housing shortage and affordability crisis can only be resolved by the construction of an adequate number of affordable housing units. Not only does rent control fail to provide new construction incentives, it almost certainly discourages new construction and other forms of supply expansion.

The Rent Control Debate

The imposition of rent control often has been justified as a necessary step to alleviate emergency housing situations often defined by vacancy rates below a certain point, say, 3 percent. Proponents argue that rent control is appropriate when rents have risen or are rising to a point at which adequate housing is beyond the means of many households, since housing is a necessity, and housing expenditures cannot easily be deferred or reduced. Without rent control, it is argued, many households will face a major deterioration in their standard of living.

Rent control advocates also point out that low vacancy rates can lead to serious abuses in the housing markets, such as rent gouging and the curtailment of needed maintenance and repairs. In areas or periods of shortage, owners may be able to gain "windfall profits" created by the shortage and unrelated to their own efforts. In such cases, rent control is seen as a device to make rents "fair" and prevent exploitation through the exercise of temporary monopoly powers by landlords due to the shortage and long lead times required for new construction.

Some have gone so far as to suggest that housing is a public good that should be controlled in the public interest, insisting that its price should be regulated like that of any public utility. Some have acknowledged long-run disadvantages but accepted rent control as necessary in the short run to help tenants with inadequate income deal with inflation and a housing shortage. Rent control in such situations is seen as buying time to create a more comprehensive housing policy.

The volume of arguments against rent control makes its popularity somewhat inexplicable. Rent control reduces the supply of new rental housing by reducing net yields relative to other investments, and it encourages the conversion of existing rental units into cooperatives and condominiums.

Rents below market level create excess demand for rental housing. Faced with an excess demand for their units and unable to raise rents, landlords often reduce maintenance and defer repairs to preserve profit margins without fear of losing tenants. When costs rise, inability to raise rents or reduce fixed capital expenditures induces landlords to curtail maintenance and repair expenditures, which reduces the quality of rental housing units and leads to a faster depreciation of the housing stock. In the long run, this leads to increased abandonments and neighborhood blight.

Rent control leads to an erosion of the local tax base by decreasing the value of rental housing properties. By reducing the income-producing ability of rental properties, rent control necessarily reduces the value of these properties. Value is also reduced because of reduced maintenance and repairs and neighborhood effects, which cause a decrease in the value of surrounding properties. The erosion of the urban tax base can lead to a reduction in municipal expenditures, which usually reduces the benefit to the urban poor the most; an increase in property tax rates; or both. A shift in property tax away from rental housing owners and onto homeowners and businesses is another possible result.

Rent control can also create severe inequities among tenants. Many well-to-do tenants who have little or no need for regulatory protection are beneficiaries of these programs. Tenants in rent-controlled units are able to reap the benefits of lower rents simply by virtue of already residing in the units. Others must either compete for the few, if any, controlled units that become available or pay the higher, uncontrolled market rents.

Policymakers describe programs that indiscriminately distribute benefits as lacking "target efficiency." Most American rent control systems fail to benefit those who most need help, for they are designed to favor long-term tenants and tend to exclude the poor, who tend to be more mobile. This aspect of rent control may also reduce the mobility of the labor force, since moving in order to get a better paying job may not be profitable if the price is a higher rent.

Other economic inefficiencies that may result are the misallocation of housing space and reduction in new construction. Rent control also encourages a mismatch between households and housing units. Many tenants, particularly older ones, may find it cheaper to remain in large, older, controlled units rather than to move into smaller units adequate for their needs. Since institutional lenders avoid units under rent control, the availability of mortgage credit for multifamily rental projects may be limited in areas subject to this regulation.

Aside from its direct effects on the housing market, rent control has many shortfalls from an administrative standpoint. These programs are expensive to administer since they deal with numerous, relatively small business entities whose financial circumstances vary and whose ability to pay for or use technical assistance is often severely limited. Finally, even when temporary controls may be justified in a serious emergency, rent control is often extremely difficult to eliminate once introduced.

The Effects of Rent Control on New Construction and the Existing Housing Stock

Since rent control is often imposed to counter price effects of a housing shortage, its effect on the construction of new rental housing units is a matter of considerable interest. Rather than helping to alleviate housing shortages, rent controls, by discouraging investment in new rental housing and encouraging the conversion of rental housing into other forms of occupancy, tend to create shortages where they did not previously exist and to make existing shortages even more severe.

A large body of literature indicates that restrictive rent controls have discouraged new construction by the private sector.[3] While there is almost universal agreement that long-term restrictive rent control leads to serious declines in new construction, the proponents of rent control argue that moderate rent controls do not have a negative impact on investments in rental housing since new construction is often excluded from regulation and since landlords are allowed what proponents describe as a "fair return."

However, it can be shown that even moderate rent control leads to a substantial decline in new construction.

Expected profit from rental investment is a function of six key variables: the expected occupancy rates, rental prices, construction costs, operating costs, revenues from reduction of tax liabilities of the investor (depreciation), and capital gains from holding the property. By reducing rents below what they otherwise would have been, rent control reduces the expected revenue of rental housing projects and the expected profitability of such ventures. Likewise, expected capital gains are reduced with rent control because of the lower values of future revenues and the more rapid deterioration of the physical structure. Lower operating (maintenance and repair) costs and higher occupancy rates produced by rent control, both of which add to expected profits, work in the opposite direction.

The possibility that rent control will be made more restrictive or be extended to other areas in the future serves to increase the riskiness of rental housing investments. This increased risk reduces expected profit by decreasing the expected rental price flow and in turn translates directly into the reduced supply of new construction, as new rental housing construction depends heavily on the profitability of such investments.

Several econometric studies indicate that new rental construction is highly responsive to rate of return.[4] These studies show generally that rental housing starts rise when rents increase, leading to higher return on investment, and fall when an increase in construction costs and operating costs cause a decline in expected returns. They show a highly sensitive housing supply system; the price elasticity of new starts with respect to real rents varies from five to fourteen between regions.

One additional variable can significantly influence the speed of adjustment and hence the supply of new construction: the availability of mortgage and construction financing, a necessary input into most new projects. These results imply that, even if developers are willing to build in rent-controlled communities, rent control can still have a negative influence on new construction if its uncertainty-generating effects cause lenders to reduce the availability of mortgage funds for new rental housing.

There are special situations in which rent control may not depress new construction. During a recession rent restrictions may become nonbinding so that they have no direct effect on supply. When growth controls or zoning are so rigid or stringent as to prevent a supply response even in the absence of rent control, rent control itself will not affect new construction.

The effects of rent control on the existing housing stock are analogous to those on new construction. As rent control depresses the rate of return on the existing stock of houses, it encourages landlords to make calculations similar to those of investors. They can be expected to take short-term actions to restore precontrol profits and to disinvest at an early opportunity.

Eventually, the rental housing stock will deteriorate qualitatively and quantitatively, as it has in a number of European countries that have had rent control in effect for an extended period of time.

The best way to encourage new construction and an adequate supply and maintenance of existing stock is to raise the rate of return to a point at which it is more in line with the overall market rate of return. A profit shortfall is the problem the market has been facing for the past five to ten years. Rent control has not solved this problem; it has only served to worsen the situation.

Reconsidering the key variables influencing the profitability of rental investment suggests there are two direct ways in which the rate of return can be increased by policy action. The first would be to raise rents and subsidize tenants, which would involve increased income transfer or income maintenance programs. As there are 23 million renter households in this country, nondiscriminatory subsidies of a magnitude adequate to stimulate new construction and maintenance of the existing rental housing stock could involve outlays of nearly $50 billion per year. Even if it used income restrictions and other criteria to qualify recipients, such a support program would still involve large sums of money, which clearly are not available in the present period of budget austerity and restructured administration priorities.

A major policy was implemented in 1981 that should stimulate new construction. The doubling of depreciation benefits for the residential multifamily assets, which were incorporated into the Economic Recovery Tax Act of 1981, have begun to have an important positive impact on the rental housing market. Reducing the tax life of these assets has reduced the tax burden (depreciation being a tax deduction against other income as well as rental income), thereby allowing the overall after-tax rate of returns to rise above pre-1981 levels. It is estimated that by shortening the present thirty-year depreciation life to fifteen years, the rate of after-tax return on residential investment properties would rise four to five percentage points.

Most policies of the 1960s and 1970s provided tremendous direct subsidies to builders for new construction rather than subsidies to tenants for rents. These policies proved extraordinarily costly and reached only a small number of those tenants with affordability problems. It would appear to be far more appropriate to give the private sector incentives through changes in the tax laws and give direct subsidies to households, avoiding the creation of layers of bureaucracy and inefficiency that are created by providing subsidies to builders through federal agencies such as the Department of Housing and Urban Development (HUD).

APPENDIX 5A

The effects of zoning and land-use controls on the supply and price of land are illustrated in Figure 5A-1. This is a vastly simplified but revealing por-

Figure 5A-1.   Price of Land and Land-Use Controls.

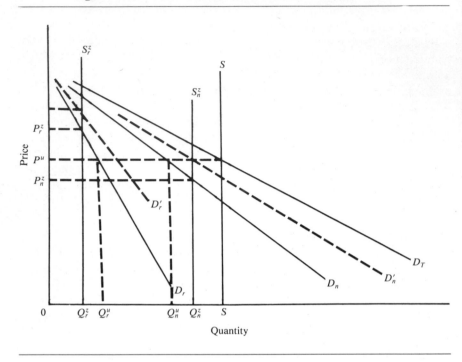

trayal of the market responses precipitated by zoning. Here, D_T is the total demand for land within a region of size S. Assuming this region neither contracts nor expands, the supply curve is vertical. D_T is the sum of the demand for land for residential (D_r) and other (D_n) uses.

In the unzoned competitive market, equilibrium occurs when total demand for land equals the total land supply available. The price of land in both submarkets is the same (P^u). Housing developers will have purchased a portion of the land equal to Q_r^u; other users will have purchased Q_n^u units of land.

Consider now the results of an administrative decision (a zoning ordinance) to limit the supply of land for residential use to S_r^z, leaving an amount S_n^z for other applications. This has the effect of creating two *apparently* independent markets. As these curves are drawn, residential purchasers "lose," paying a higher price (P_r^z) for less land ($Q_r^z = S_r^z$), and other purchasers or land users "win," paying less (P_n^z) for more ($Q_n^z = S_n^z$).[5]

In fact, these markets are not independent because of interdependencies between residential and nonresidential uses of land. Presumably, the greater number of amenities in this region would attract additional people and firms

Figure 5A–2.   Price of Housing and Land-Use Controls.

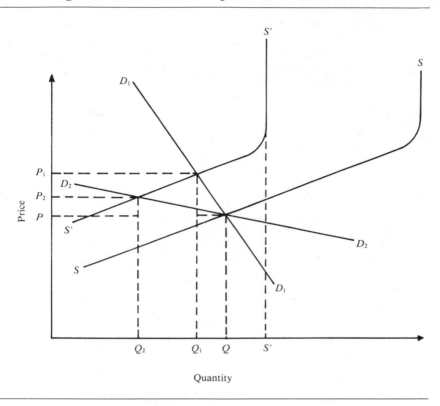

to the area. The additional population growth and employment opportunities would then stimulate residential demand (D_t') and produce still higher prices for this group under zoning if sufficient nearby housing space were not available.

    Figure 5A–2 illustrates the impact of restrictive zoning regulations on the new housing market. The restriction of residentially zoned land — which, as illustrated in Figure 5A–2, serves to increase the price of residential land, minimum lot size and floor area requirements, architectural controls, delays, and administrative work caused by zoning ordinances — works to increase the costs per unit of building new housing. Graphically, this implies an upward shift of the supply curve from SS to $S'S'$. Also, the restriction of residentially zoned land means the supply curve becomes vertical earlier, and the need to require costly variances and rezonings to develop in certain areas means the supply curve also starts getting steeper at a lower Q. For a given set of zoning regulations, the effect on the price of new housing will depend mainly on the price elasticity of demand for new housing. As seen in Figure 5A-2, for a fairly inelastic demand curve, such as $D_1 D_1$, zoning restrictions will cause a large price increase, and for a fairly elastic demand curve, such as $D_2 D_2$, the price increase will not be as large.

NOTES

1. Stephen B. Seidel, *Housing Costs and Government Regulations* (New Brunswick, N.J.: Center for Urban Policy Research, 1978), p. 135; Sherman T. Maisel, "A Theory of Fluctuations in Residential Construction Starts," *American Economic Review* 53 (June 1963): 359–83; David E. Dowall, "The Effect of Land Use and Environmental Regulations on Housing Costs," *Policy Studies Journal* 8 (1979): 277–88; Robert C. Ellickson, "Suburban Growth Controls: An Economic and Legal Analysis," *The Yale Law Journal* 86 (January 1977): 385–511; Seymour I. Schwartz et al., "The Effect of Growth Management on New Housing Price: Petaluma, California" (Davis, Calif.: Institute of Governmental Affairs, University of California, 1979).

2. The data are described in Kenneth Rosen and Larry Katz, "The Impact of Land-Use Controls on House Prices in California," Center for Real Estate and Urban Economics, Working Paper 80–13.

3. W. Block and E. Olsen, eds., *Rent Control: Myths and Realities* (Vancouver: The Fraser Institute, 1981); Frank de Leeuw and Nkanta F. Ekanem, "The Supply of Rental Housing," *American Economic Review* 61 (December 1971): 806–17; Frank de Leeuw and Nkanta F. Ekanem, "Time Lags in the Rental Housing Market," *Urban Studies* 10 (February 1973): 39–68; Harvey S. Rosen and Kenneth T. Rosen, "Federal Taxes and Homeownership: Evidence from Time Series," *Journal of Political Economy* 88 (February 1980): 59–75; Lawrence B. Smith, "A Note on the Price Adjustment Mechanism for Rental Housing," *American Economic Review* 64 (June 1974): 478–81.

4. Kenneth T. Rosen, "A Regional Model of Multifamily Housing Starts," *Journal of American Real Estate and Urban Economics Association* 7, no. 1 (Spring 1979).

5. The total revenues generated by property sales under zoning could be higher or lower, depending on the price elasticity of demand in each market. Similarly, the municipality itself could be either a "winner" or a "loser" under zoning, depending on the nature of its revenue generation mechanisms, or tax structure.

Chapter 6

The Restructuring of the Housing Finance System

In the late 1970s a major restructuring of the traditional housing finance system began. Regulation of deposit interest rates at federally chartered financial institutions has been virtually eliminated. New types of deposit accounts calculated to restore savings flows to thrifts have become common. Secondary-market transactions and passthrough certificates, whereby mortgage originators sell their loans to nontraditional mortgage lenders, are increasingly used as tools to generate cash, which, in turn, can be used to originate additional mortgages. An array of new mortgage instruments — such as adjustable-rate, graduated-payment, and growing-equity loans — that take into account variations in the household life cycle and income circumstances are now an important supplement to the traditional fixed-rate fixed-payment mortgage.

These innovations have arisen in an environment characterized by periodic bouts of disintermediation, the mortgage credit gap, the affordability crisis for first-time buyers, the profitability crisis for lenders, and volatile interest rates. They represent a large change in institutional priorities and policies.

In the long run the movement from a highly regulated to a market-oriented housing finance system should produce a more adequate and stable flow of funds to the housing sector. However, the possibility that this change-over can be made in a smooth and nondisruptive manner is highly questionable. There is substantial potential for a crisis in the housing finance system, which may turn the transition from a regulated to a deregulated financial structure into a catastrophe.

TRADITIONAL LENDERS

Deregulation of the Deposit Market

The major characteristic of the consumer deposit market from 1965 to 1978 was the rigid interest rate ceilings placed on deposit accounts. Under Regulation Q and related provisions, the maximum interest rate that thrift institutions and commercial banks (CBs) could pay on passbook and term deposits was set by the agency responsible for regulating them. Thus, the Federal Reserve Board (FRB), the Federal Home Loan Bank Board (FHLBB), and the Federal Deposit Insurance Corporation (FDIC) set the maximum rates that can be paid by CBs, savings and loan associations (SLAs), and mutual savings banks (MSBs), respectively. Under the Depository Institutions Deregulation and Monetary Control Act passed in March 1980, authority to set maximum interest rates payable on deposits was centralized in the Depository Institutions Deregulation Committee (DIDC). The DIDC was composed of the chairmen of each of the three regulatory agencies (FRB, FHLBB, and FDIC), the secretary of the Treasury, and the director of the National Credit Union Administration. The DIDC was directed to phase out all deposit interest rate ceilings by 1986 in an orderly and nondisruptive manner.

Initially, deposit rate ceilings were imposed because of fear of "predatory competition" and the desire to stimulate home mortgage lending. Predatory competition describes the situation in which financial institutions compete for consumer deposits without regard to profit and solvency constraints. Many economists argue that this fear is groundless in a competitive environment and serves merely as a rationale for providing a sheltered environment for the regulated financial institutions. Valid or not, the predatory competition argument was utilized in 1965 when interest rate ceilings were imposed on SLA deposit accounts in response to pressure on regulators by East Coast institutions facing tough competition by West Coast SLAs seeking funds to meet the burgeoning demand for mortgage credit in a rapidly growing California housing market.

The second rationale for the imposition of deposit rate ceilings on the housing finance system derived from the desire to encourage home mortgage lending. Institutions investing primarily in residential mortgage loans were allowed to offer a higher return to depositors than were those primarily engaged in other kinds of lending. The differential interest rate for thrifts was meant to create a captive source of funds for the housing industry. By paying a higher interest rate than CBs on deposits the thrifts presumably would capture a larger share of household deposits, which, in turn, would be lent for residential mortgages.

Despite their dubious origin, the regulations were fairly successful throughout the 1960s and early 1970s; the market share of deposits for SLAs increased, and on average, mortgage credit was available at a surprisingly low cost relative to the costs of other kinds of long-term credit. There were, however, three periods of major disruption in the flow of mortgage credit, corresponding to periods when market interest rates were substantially above ceiling interest rates. As shown in Chapter 4, cyclical instability in housing activity was substantially exacerbated by this regulatory environment — leading to periodic credit crunches and housing recessions as well as overbuilding.

In the late 1970s the regulated financial structure began to look increasingly vulnerable. High and volatile interest and inflation rates combined with rigid deposit interest rate ceilings made deposits at regulated financial institutions unattractive. The sophistication of depositors seemed to grow with each increase in market interest rates. Investments in Treasury bills and money market mutual funds became increasingly common. The major negative consequences of the ceilings increasingly fell on unsophisticated, often elderly, savers. As disintermediation proceeded, the inequity of this Regulation Q tax became more and more apparent to both the public and politicians.

The initial response of regulators to the eroding effectiveness of Regulation Q ceilings was piecemeal deregulation. In a classic case of price discrimination, ceilings on short-term, larger deposit accounts were relaxed. In June 1978 regulated financial institutions were first authorized to offer money market certificates (MMCs) with interest rates tied to the rate determined at the most recent six-month Treasury bill auction. Until May 1979 thrift institutions continued to pay 0.25 percent more than CBs; since then, the differential has been eliminated when the Treasury bill rate is above 9 percent. The MMCs require a $10,000 minimum deposit for a six-month period.

In January 1980 financial institutions were also authorized to offer variable ceiling deposits with maturities of two and a half years or more — small savers certificates, or SSCs. In March 1980 a temporary ceiling interest rate of 12 percent was placed on these accounts, effectively making them a below-market account. In August 1981 they were fully deregulated.

Finally, in December 1982, with the introduction of the money market deposit account (MMDA), regulated financial institutions were allowed to offer market rates on virtually all short-term deposits. MMDAs have no interest rate ceiling and require only a $2,500 deposit. They also require depositors to write no more than three checks per month, which makes them quite similar to money market mutual funds.

Judged by consumer acceptance, the MMC, SSC, and MMDA accounts have been major successes: by mid-1984 nearly 75 percent of all thrift deposits

Table 6-1. Share of Deposit Flows by Type of Institution (percentage distribution).

Year	Thrifts	Commercial Banks	Money Market Mutual Funds
1971	49.6	50.3	–
1972	51.5	48.4	–
1973	36.4	53.5	–
1974	21.2	76.4	2.4
1975	45.7	54.0	0.3
1976	64.8	34.8	0.1
1977	41.0	58.9	0.1
1978	35.7	59.5	4.8
1979	34.2	37.7	28.1
1980	20.9	66.4	12.7
1981	8.0	31.3	60.7
1982	21.9	64.9	13.2
1983[a]	24[a]	62[a]	−33[a]

[a] First half of 1983 in billions of dollars; because of negative number, a percentage cannot be calculated.

Source: Raw data from Federal Reserve Board, various tables.

were in these accounts. Judged from the view of providing an effective and equitable source of mortgage credit, the results are not as clear.

The introduction of MMCs succeeded in educating and sensitizing the public to money market returns. This created not only a rapid growth in MMCs but an even more rapid growth in money market mutual funds. Thus, the MMC had a mixed effect on the deposit shares of thrift institutions. As Table 6-1 shows, during normal periods thrifts have attracted about 50 percent of all consumer deposits. During 1979 and 1980 their share dropped to 20 to 30 percent despite the success of the MMC. Thus, their deposit share was roughly similar to that during a typical disintermediation period such as 1973-74. In 1981 the situation deteriorated far more dramatically. The thrift share fell to less than 8 percent as a result of the overwhelming dominance of the money market mutual funds, which captured over 60 percent of the deposit market. In 1982 the thrift share rebounded to 22 percent primarily due to the introduction of the MMDA in December 1982. In 1983 the shift of deposits from money funds led to extremely large inflows for both thrifts and CBs.

The piecemeal deregulation that led to the MMC and the SSC has not been particularly effective in moderating the housing cycle and at best can be said to have been a holding action. On the other hand, there is good reason to believe that full deregulation of all deposits, which occurred with the MMDA, will allow the thrifts to compete more effectively with money market funds. Unless broad-scale competition with all other institutions is possible, it will be difficult to ensure a stable and adequate supply of mortgage credit from traditional sources.

Partial deregulation of deposit accounts has, however, had some very negative short-run consequences. By raising the cost and shortening the maturity of deposit liabilities, they have put thrift institutions in a continued profit squeeze due to the predominance of fixed-rate, long-term mortgages in their asset portfolios, which has reduced their effectiveness as mortgage lenders. While the full deregulation of the deposit market will mitigate the periodic credit rationing that the housing market has experienced, it has exposed depository institutions to even more interest rate risk than in the past. By exacerbating the maturity imbalance problem, the new deregulated deposit accounts could put SLAs in an even worse profitability crisis during the next period of high interest rates.

Changing Sources of Mortgage Credit

Deregulation of the deposit market has had a large effect on the role of traditional lenders in the mortgage market. There has been a dramatic shift within the institutional lending community in terms of *net* mortgage extension (change in net holdings of mortgages). Table 6–2 shows the startling drop in the SLA and CB mortgage shares and the sharp rise in the role of the secondary-market transactions (represented by mortgage pools) and in households' provision of mortgage credit (through seller second mortgages).

Table 6–2. Sources of Net Extension of Home Mortgage Credit (percentage).

	1977	1978	1979	1980	1981	1982
Households	5.9	10.2	13.5	21.4	26.9	23.6
State and local government	0.2	1.8	4.0	8.2	7.7	4.1
Sponsored credit agencies	0.5	8.0	7.7	7.9	6.6	11.5
Mortgage pools	16.1	11.0	18.3	19.5	18.5	50.3
Commercial banks	19.4	21.3	16.8	11.4	16.0	18.4
Savings institutions	56.6	45.3	35.2	28.5	18.9	−9.2
Life insurance	−1.4	−0.3	1.5	1.9	−0.8	0.4
Pension funds	0.0	0.3	0.3	0.4	0.4	0.0
Other	2.7	0.4	2.7	0.8	5.8	5.0

Source: Federal Reserve Board, *Flow of Funds Accounts,* Federal Reserve Board Annual Revisions, various issues.

The table also shows the small but increasing role in the mortgage market played by sponsored credit agencies and state and local government (through mortgage revenue bonds). The reduction in SLA market shares of all mortgage lending results from a declining share of consumer deposits and recent FHLBB actions easing restrictions on the SLA asset portfolio. Thus, the short-term phenomena highlighted in Table 6-2 are symptomatic of a long-run shift in the mortgage market, creating a gap in mortgage supply from the conventional thrift industry sources.

The mortgage market will adjust to the diminishing role of SLAs in mortgage originations in a number of ways. Mortgage rates will be driven up because of the excess demand conditions. As a result the credit gap is likely to produce higher relative mortgage interest rates and lower loan-to-value ratios (higher down payment requirements). More attractive mortgage terms should induce nonthrift institutions to make more mortgage loans. Thus, pension funds and life insurance companies (LICs) will increasingly purchase the attractively priced new mortgages as they become available. Thrift institutions themselves will alter their behavior if normal sources of cash flow are insufficient to meet mortgage demand. In particular, thrifts will increase borrowing from the Federal Home Loan Banks System and other sources, including mortgage-backed bonds. A strong continued movement toward secondary-market sales is likely, both in a direct form and through "mortgage pool" or passthrough securities and collateralized mortgage obligations (CMOs). This trend, in which the ultimate holders of mortgages are different from the originators, is likely to accelerate in the 1980s. It will be accommodated, in part, by the role of the quasi-federal agencies as guarantors of these mortgage pools.

In addition to these institutional adjustments there have also been major adjustments by homebuyers, sellers, and builders to the "new mortgage realities" of the early 1980s. Two different "creative financing" arrangements have grown phenomenally. The first is the "buydown" of mortgage interest rates for a period of two to five years by a new homebuilder. Essentially, the builder is reducing his buyer's cost for a period of time by paying the buyer's interest. After this period the borrower's income will presumably have risen, because of inflation and real growth in productivity, so that he or she can afford market rate financing. Because of the financing burden it places on builders this technique can be expected to increase the price of a new home.

The second arrangement concerns the financing of existing houses and often involves two elements: an assumption (transfer) of an existing low-rate mortgage loan and a second mortgage loan by the seller at below-market prices. The extent of this technique for financing existing home sales can be seen from Table 6-3. Column (1) shows the volume of new loan originations by all institutional lenders for existing homes. Column (2) shows the product of existing home sales, house prices, and median loan-to-value

Table 6-3. Creative Financing.

Year	All Institution Mortgage Originations Existing Homes ($ billions) (1)	Value of Existing Home Sales[a] ($ billions) (2)	Percentage Creatively Financed[b] (3)
1970	22.986	29.456	21.964
1971	37.332	41.756	10.596
1972	50.031	51.517	2.884
1973	51.157	57.745	11.409
1974	43.377	58.888	26.340
1975	53.328	70.878	24.761
1976	80.627	95.424	15.507
1977	115.550	131.301	11.996
1978	127.021	166.138	23.545
1979	126.083	181.813	30.652
1980	84.624	158.993	46.775
1981	60.910	138.040	55.875
1982	64.735	114.997	43.707
1983[c]	28.100	32.500	13.400

[a] Sales × average price × median loan-value ratio.

[b] [1 − (column 1/column 2)].

[c] First quarter of 1983.

Source: Raw data obtained from the Department of Housing and Urban Development, the U.S. Bureau of the Census, and the National Association of Realtors.

ratios. Column (3) shows a ratio of Column (2) to Column (1), illustrating the amount of noninstitutional mortgage lending and mortgage lending that involves the assumption of old mortgage loans and seller second loans. These data show that in the early 1980s a majority of the financing of existing homes has not involved new mortgages from lending institutions but instead has involved creative financing by households. The trend toward creative financing was reversed in 1983 due to massive deposit flows into regulated financial intermediaries and a sharp drop in mortgage interest rates.

THE ROLE OF THE FEDERAL AND QUASI-FEDERAL AGENCIES IN THE RESTRUCTURED HOUSING FINANCE SYSTEM

The restructuring of the private financial system has significantly changed the traditional roles of key government and quasi-government agencies.

Once the liability structure of financial institutions is completely deregulated they will be able to compete for deposit funds on the basis of yield to savers. This in turn should reduce the periodic spells of disintermediation from mortgage-lending institutions, which has been the main cause of non-price rationing of mortgage credit and cyclical instability in housing production. Of course, interest rate fluctuations might then create a new form of instability that the agencies could try to moderate.

In addition to combating the likely continued instability in housing production, the agencies will also be called upon to address the mortgage credit gap described earlier. The excess demand for mortgage credit and the Reagan administration's desire to reduce the guarantor role of the Federal Housing Administration (FHA) and Government National Mortgage Association (GNMA) will require the remaining agencies to devise an innovative set of programs to facilitate the required supply of mortgage credit in the 1980s.

Agency Countercyclical Mortgage Assistance Policies[1]

Public policy toward the cyclical instability in residential construction is based on the premise that cyclical instability in mortgage lending causes fluctuations in housing activity. Stabilizing mortgage credit supply has consequently been a major policy since the mid-1960s. The establishment of the Federal Home Loan Mortgage Corporation (FHLMC), the reorganization of the Federal National Mortgage Association (FNMA), and the reorientation of the GNMA were, in part, attempts to safeguard mortgage and housing markets from general financial restraint. The dramatic growth of the activity of these agencies has also made the federal government an integral part of the mortgage credit and housing production system.

In addition to the role of these agencies, since mid-1978 public policy toward cyclical instability has taken a surprising new turn. Following the long-standing recommendations of housing economists, the deregulation of the housing finance system is now nearly completed. The introduction of the first MMC and the recent introduction of the MMDA have substantially mitigated the inflexibility of Regulation Q ceilings. In addition, the passage of the federal override of state usury law ceilings has alleviated the negative consequences of these market restraints. Finally, the widespread use of variable-rate mortgage and the removal of other asset restrictions from SLAs will enhance their ability to deal with a volatile economic climate. As a result of these actions, federal policy appears to be directly confronting the historic cause of the cyclical stability problem—the supply rationing of mortgage credit.

The establishment of the public intermediaries (the FHLBB, FNMA, FHLMC, and to some extent GNMA) can be viewed as an attempt to direct capital toward SLAs and other mortgage-creating institutions during periods of financial restraint, in an effort to offset the disintermediation phenomena experienced by financing institutions. Figure 6–1 depicts these processes. The federal agencies have been given a variety of instruments to attract and direct capital, including direct subsidies and indirect subsidies in the form of federal guarantees of agency securities.

There are two basic mechanisms by which the federal agencies can influence the housing and mortgage markets. The FHLBB, reacting to conditions in the housing and mortgage markets, makes advances or loans to the SLAs, which can then expand their holdings of mortgages in excess of their inflow of savings deposits. These advances are analogous to borrowings of CBs from the Federal Reserve System (FRS), except that, unlike these FRS "discount window" borrowings, they are often of an intermediate- or long-term nature, thus supplementing the supply of long-term mortgage credit. The advances are financed by the sale of FHLBB securities in the open market.

The second mechanism enhances the ability of SLAs and other intermediaries to acquire liquidity by selling their holdings of mortgages on the secondary market. Funds derived from these transactions can be used to acquire new mortgages. The FNMA can purchase Federal Housing Administration (FHA)–Veterans' Administration (VA) or conventional mortgages from the mortgage bankers, SLAs, and other mortgage originators, financing the purchase through the sale of its own securities in the open market. The FHLMC can purchase conventional mortgage loans from SLAs and mortgage bankers, with financing derived primarily through the sale of mortgage-backed securities. In the mid-1970s the GNMA was also authorized to purchase conventional and FHA-VA mortgages at below-market interest rates, with the mortgages then being resold to the FNMA or FHLMC. Through the Emergency Home Purchase Act of 1974 the GNMA became a major direct countercyclical support program in the housing recession of 1974–75. Unfortunately, because of opposition from the Reagan administration, the GNMA was not allowed to function in a countercyclical capacity in the 1981–82 housing recession.

These mechanisms have two features in common. They allow mortgage-creating institutions to make loans in amounts that exceed their current cash flows, composed of net deposit flows and repayments of existing loans, and they require the agencies to generate funds on the open capital market to finance their activities.

Until 1982 the two major secondary-market agencies, the FNMA and the FHLMC, functioned in a similar fashion. Believing in the efficiency of

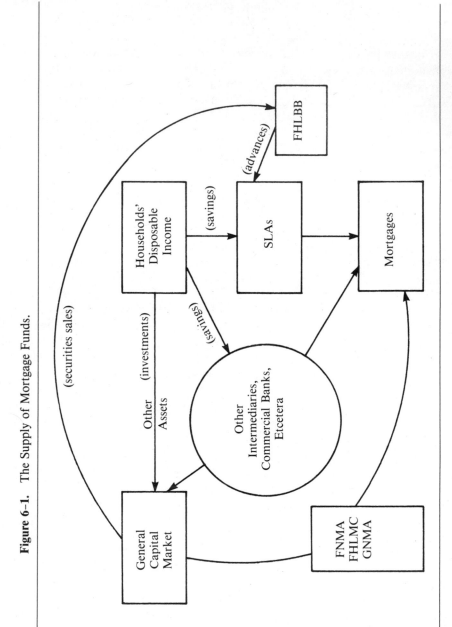

Figure 6-1. The Supply of Mortgage Funds.

market mechanisms, both agencies used an auction system to determine the volume of their activity in their major mortgage-purchasing programs. Bimonthly those individuals and organizations wishing to sell mortgages to the FNMA and FHLMC specified the dollar volume of mortgages they wished to sell and the effective yield they were offering on that volume. The agencies then determined the volume and cut-off yield of acceptable bids. Where the cut-off bid was set critically determined the amount of money pumped into the mortgage market. Both agencies considered two major factors in determining this cut-off bid. First, they examined their expected cost of funds to ensure themselves an adequate profit margin (in the case of the FNMA) or solvency margin (in the case of the FHLMC). Second, they considered the credit needs of the market and presumably attempted to offset shortages or excesses of mortgage funds.

While the demand for FNMA and FHLMC commitments was determined by those offering mortgages in the auction, the ultimate supply and volume of market support was determined by the number of offers accepted by the agencies, and therefore, by the cut-off yield. If these agencies were reacting in a countercyclical fashion they should reduce their "profit and solvency margins" during periods of credit restraint and thus accept additional mortgages. During periods of financial ease they should increase profit and solvency margins and so marginally reduce the quantity of mortgages they accept during those periods.

Once the volume of acceptances was determined by the agency it issued a commitment to the offering lender. The commitment provided the lender with an option to sell the specified quantity of mortgage loans to the agency at a specified interest rate over periods ranging from several weeks to over a year. The lender then either "took down" the commitment, in which case it sold mortgages to the agency, or canceled the commitment. The FHLMC functioned somewhat differently in that the "take-downs" of its commitments were mandatory.

In the past two years both the FNMA and the FHLMC have replaced the auction system with a system of posted yields to which the lender can react. The agencies feel this provides them with a quicker ability to react to market conditions.

The GNMA's countercyclical mechanism functioned in a different fashion. Its activities were a direct function of the actions of Congress and the Department of Housing and Urban Development (HUD). Congress passed the Emergency Home Purchase Assistance Act in October 1974, authorizing the GNMA to purchase up to $7.75 billion of single-family home mortgages at interest rates ranging from 7.5 to 8.5 percent. The GNMA was authorized to enter into a commitment contract with a private lender to purchase an FHA-VA or conventional loan within a one-year period after the commitment was made. The GNMA financed its purchase of mortgages through borrowings from the Treasury and revenues from the sale of previously purchased mortgages. From October 1974 to August 1975 the GNMA released $7.93 billion in mortgage commitments. These commitments resulted in mortgage purchases of $6.4 billion.

The GNMA's involvement in countercyclical policy was essentially a one-time action authorized during a period of severe recession in the housing industry. An attempt to reactivate the GNMA countercyclical program in 1981 was strongly resisted by a deficit conscious administration and Congress. Whether this program will be reinstituted in future periods of cyclical decline in housing markets is uncertain.

If the FNMA, FHLBB, FHLMC, and GNMA do attempt to serve as a stabilizing influence in the housing and mortgage markets, there are two aspects of their activity that must be assessed. It is first desirable to examine the extent to which their reactions to market events are "correct" in a countercyclical sense. It is then necessary to examine the overall effectiveness of their activities in moderating fluctuations in mortgage lending and in residential construction activity. To assess these two aspects of FNMA, FHLBB, FHLMC, and GNMA activity, several econometric models of housing and mortgage markets have been constructed. The models estimate housing starts, mortgage flows to thrift institutions, and open market interest rates.[2]

The agencies have developed a set of institutional mechanisms that are highly responsive to the demands of mortgage market participants. The market systems of the FNMA and the FHLMC, the advance mechanisms of the FHLBB, and the emergency countercyclical program of the GNMA all responded to the cyclical credit needs of the mortgage and housing markets in a strongly countercyclical fashion. With respect to savings flows to thrift institutions — the usual leading indicator of housing and mortgage market activity — all the agencies appeared strongly countercyclical. When individual savers disintermediate, transferring their funds from thrift institutions to other assets and intermediaries, the FNMA, FHLBB, FHLMC, and GNMA appeared to rush in and divert funds from the general capital market back to the mortgage-creating institutions.

In the 1970s the activities of these agencies were basically correct in a countercyclical sense. That is, they increased mortgage acquisitions (for the FNMA, FHLMC, and GNMA) or advances made (for the FHLBB) during trough periods in housing activity and decreased them during periods of peak activity in the housing market. Prior to 1968 the activities of these agencies were not clearly countercyclical and in some cases were procyclical. Table 6-4 illustrates and characterizes the countercyclical activity of these agencies.

In the 1980–81 decline in housing activity the agencies did not appear to react in a countercyclical fashion. They all put less money into the market in 1980 than during the peak years of 1978–79. In partial defense of the agencies, there were extremely unsettled conditions prevailing in the spring of 1980. Mortgage interest rates were high, and plentiful flows of funds resulted from the new MMCs. This reduced the demand for nonsubsidized credit from the agencies. The extremely distressed condition of the FNMA itself was also influential. The FNMA, because of a portfolio imbalance problem similar to the SLAs', sustained large losses in 1980, 1981, and 1982. Regardless of cause, however, the agencies were not acting in a strong countercyclical fashion in 1980–81. Only by early 1982 had the FNMA and FHLMC begun to pump large amounts of money into the mortgage market.

Limitations on agency effectiveness arise from a number of sources. The nature of the institutional relationship of the agencies to the mortgage market constrains their ability to influence the market. They are largely dependent on lender initiative in making use of advances or the secondary mortgage market. SLAs cannot be forced to demand advances, even though rate policies may encourage their use, and they cannot be forced to use advances for mortgage purposes, as opposed to general liquidity purposes. Likewise, the FNMA, FHLMC, and GNMA cannot force lenders to sell mortgages, even though interest rate policies can encourage such sales.

Their use of interest rate policies is, however, limited by the nature of the organizations. The FNMA is a profit-making company and so cannot be expected to sacrifice profitability completely in order to meet a cyclical stability goal. During periods of cyclical tightness the FNMA faces the same yield differential problem confronted by other intermediaries. The FNMA has attempted to counteract this problem by lengthening the average life of its debt to match its assets and liabilities better, but this does not alter the basic fact that one of the FNMA's major goals is, of necessity, profitability. In fact, the FNMA appears to have sacrificed some profitability in order to meet a countercyclical goal—a sacrifice measured by a reduction in the FNMA's profit margin during periods of financial restraint. During periods of credit ease, however, it does not appear that the FNMA attempts to slow down its rate of mortgage acquisition by expanding its profit margin.[3]

The FHLMC, while not a profit-making organization (though it does report earnings and pay dividends to its Federal Home Banks stockholders), is influenced by similar desires—a solvency constraint that may limit the extent to which advances and commitments below borrowing costs can be made. It appears, however, that the FHLMC has made no attempt to alter its solvency margin in a countercyclical fashion. These contrasting reactions are surprising, given that the FHLMC is a public agency and the FNMA essentially a private one.[4] In the fall of 1983, following the lead of new FHLBB Chairman Ed Gray, the FHLMC reduced profit spreads to stimulate mortgage lending.

Table 6-4.   Actions of the FNMA, FHLBB, FHLMC, and GNMA Near Peak or Trough Periods.

Approximate Turning Point Dates in Housing (year:quarter)	FNMA New Commitments of Mortgages by Quarter ($ millions)					Character-ization of Actions[a]
1965:4 peak	120	226	742	772	413	correct
1966:4 trough	413	322	412	113	283	incorrect
1968:4 peak	623	807	712	1,036	1,553	correct
1969:4 trough	1,553	2,087	1,956	2,349	2,121	correct
1972:1 peak	2,634	4,042	1,683	2,518	1,933	correct
1974:3 trough[b]	2,245	3,826	3,373	1,310	922	correct
1977:4 peak	3,167	1,252	3,205	5,315	7,075	mixed
1980:2 trough	3,267	2,332	1,339	2,984	1,389	incorrect
1981:4 trough	2,294	3,866	2,504	3,897	5,615	mixed

	FHLBB (changes in advances outstanding)[c]					
1965:4 peak	838	216	195	−310	1,095	correct
1966:4 trough	1,095	392	−240	−1,759	−873	incorrect
1968:4 peak	619	138	234	70	1,081	correct
1969:4 trough	1,081	1,228	1,349	396	475	correct
1972:1 peak	395	299	−1,946	84	662	correct
1974:3 trough	−150	2,674	3,129	1,033	−3,640	correct
1977:4 peak	1,267	1,305	3,039	1,082	3,840	incorrect
1980:2 trough	2,819	1,973	−1,796	1,929	4,481	mixed to incorrect
1981:4 trough	6,517	8,018	932	855	3,291	correct

	GNMA (new commitments)					
1974:3 trough	520	1,890	1,960	3,630	4,210	correct but slow
1977:4 peak 1980:2 trough 1981:4 trough			− no program −			incorrect

	FHLMC (new commitments)					
1974:3 trough	670	2,510	1,270	90	90	correct
1977:4 peak	760	−2	−180	−110	760	correct
1980:2 trough	924	679	1,257	1,396	527	mixed to correct
1981:4 trough	541	1,538	4,048	6,368	8,682	correct

Despite the limited active policy response by the FHLMC and the somewhat constrained response during periods of credit ease by the GNMA, the overall design of the mortgage commitment mechanism makes both agencies appear strongly countercyclical. It is the strong response of demanders to the availability of credit from these sources that gives the agencies their countercyclical impact.

Only the GNMA, a government agency, did not face profitability or solvency constraints, and during the 1974–75 credit crunch it assisted the mortgage and housing markets — at a cost to taxpayers of $412 million.[5]

The most important limitation on the activity of these agencies is related to the general equilibrium effects of their activities. The FNMA, FHLMC, FHLBB, and GNMA influence not only the supply and price of mortgages but, through their borrowing activities, also the cost of funds in the general capital market. When they issue securities to finance mortgage purchases they increase overall market interest rates, thus contributing to the disintermediation problem. This in turn decreases their effect on the mortgage market by reducing private mortgage availability. Therefore, the net impact of any injection of funds on the availability of mortgages depends on the response of market interest rates to incremental borrowing and on the response of savings flows to changes in free market interest rates. In addition, the injection of resources into the construction sector might intensify inflationary pressures, causing further upward pressure on interest rate levels.

The sum of these general equilibrium effects can be estimated using simulation techniques with a version of the econometric model mentioned previously. Two sets of simulations were run. The first represents a period when credit rationing was present in the mortgage market. The second represents a "nonrationing" regime. In both cases the agencies were assumed to provide $1 billion of mortgages per month starting in month four. It was assumed that these activities continued for a six-month period. Of course, neither simulation represents the "true" effects of these agencies but should be viewed as depicting a likely range of consequences in the housing, mortgage, and capital markets of the agency programs. (For more details see note 6.)

Notes to Table 6–4.

   [a] For FNMA, a correct stabilization policy would be to increase rate of mortgage commitments during trough periods. For FHLBB, advances outstanding should be increased during trough period and decreased during peak period if a correct stabilization policy is implemented.

   [b] The actual trough of the cycle was 1975:1, but the market was experiencing major distress beginning in 1973:4.

   [c] Figures shown for turning point and two quarters on either side of turning point in housing starts. The turning point is set in boldface.

   Source: Federal Reserve Bulletin.

The net contribution of these agencies to mortgage supply appears to be substantially less than their gross injection of mortgage funds. Only 17 to 34 percent of their gross mortgage fund provision is translated into additional mortgage provisions.[6] The higher estimate includes the dollar value of new housing starts and existing home sales stimulated during the rationing regime. The lower estimate includes the dollar value of starts stimulated during a nonrationing regime.

This small net impact is due primarily to the adverse influence of agency borrowing on open market interest rates and therefore on private flows to thrift institutions. In addition, other financial intermediaries reallocate their portfolios away from the mortgage market in response to a relative decline in the mortgage rate. The combination of these indirect supply and demand effects offsets a major portion of the effect of these agencies. Table 6-5 highlights these counteracting effects. These programs initially reduce mortgage interest rates and raise housing starts and mortgage lending. However, they also raise other market interest rates and reduce deposit flows to SLAs, thus offsetting part of their initial positive impact. Therefore, while the activities of the agencies are clearly countercyclical, both institutional and market limitations greatly reduce their ability to moderate cyclical fluctuations in residential construction.

While admitting this general equilibrium constraint, there are additional procedures that the agencies could undertake to improve their cyclical responsiveness and enhance their effectiveness. In particular, the FNMA could be more aggressive during periods of credit glut by further reducing commitment volume at such times. The FNMA appears to lower rather than raise its required yield spread during periods of credit glut. The FHLMC could increase the demand for commitments during periods of credit tightness by cutting its "solvency margin" more than it presently does. The GNMA's countercyclical mechanism could be made more responsive if it were triggered by market mechanisms rather than awaiting congressional and executive branch authorizations. Finally, the countercyclical activities of all these agencies would be improved if there were increased interagency coordination. Improved coordination would assist in forecasting and identifying cyclical distress; allow a better determination of aggregate dollar levels of assistance required; and perhaps eliminate costly duplication in administrative functions, which would suggest, perhaps, a consolidation of countercyclical functions in one or two agencies rather than the present four.

Because of the deregulation of the housing finance system, to achieve a strongly countercyclical effect these agencies might have to react to market events in a different way in the 1980s. Since nonprice credit rationing should be less of a problem for the housing finance system in the 1980s, the agencies will have to counteract the effects of interest rate volatility on the housing sector. This will be a far more difficult task, as it requires some type of

Table 6–5. Simulation Experiments Changes from Base Run of Model (cumulative from date of policy shock).

	Mortgage Rate (percentage points)	Mortgage Loans Outstanding SLAs ($ billions)	Savings SLAs ($ billions)	Housing Starts (thousands of units)	Value of Housing Starts	T-Bill Rate (percentage points)	3-5 Year Bond (percentage points)
Supply side (rationing period)							
4 months	−0.252	+3.206	−0.256	+53.46	+2.15	+0.32	+0.18
7 months	−0.262	+3.882	−1.581	+84.66	+3.44	+0.63	+0.26
12 months	−0.033	+0.415	−3.451	+101.10	+4.17	+0.24	+0.06
Supply side (nonrationing)							
4 months	−0.124	+1.076	−0.231	+7.62	+0.372	+0.27	+0.16
7 months	−0.154	+1.642	−1.670	+39.06	+1.924	+0.66	+0.28
12 months	+0.06	−0.967	−3.739	+62.63	+3.093	+0.31	+0.086

Source: Jaffee–Rosen, *Journal of Finance*, June 1978.

countercyclical subsidy program. A program modeled on the same principle as the "builder buydowns" or owner-provided second "balloon" mortgage at below-market rates could be effective. Both of these concepts provide temporary subsidies to the buyer, usually for a period of one to three years, thus balancing the impact of high interest rates. The FNMA initated the purchase of buydown mortgages in 1981. The countercyclical mortgage subsidy legislation introduced by Senator Richard Lugar in 1982 was an attempt to implement such a policy.

The Agencies and the Mortgage Credit Gap

The extraordinary secular increase in the demand for mortgage credit, which began in the late 1970s and will accelerate in the mid- to late 1980s, creates an important new role for the mortgage agencies: attracting nontraditional mortgage lenders to the mortgage market.

In recent years the use of government-backed mortgage securities has undergone a virtual explosion of activity. The GNMA passthrough security program began in 1970 as an attempt to attract nontraditional mortgage lenders to the mortgage market. The rapid entry of the FHLMC and FNMA into the passthrough security guarantee market has opened a new range of opportunities for the conventional mortgage lender. This growth in the passthrough securities market has sharply accelerated the trend toward an "unbundling" (separating origination, servicing, and holding functions) of services offered by the traditional mortgage lenders.[7]

A mortgage passthrough certificate represents an ownership interest in a pool of mortgage loans. The pool results from the sale of assets by mortgage originators, and the certificate provides the holder with regularly scheduled monthly payments of principal and interest. In addition, any prepayments of mortgage loans in the pool are also "passed through" to the certificate holder. Thus, because of the possibility of unscheduled loan repayments, there is not a fixed schedule of payments on the passthrough certificate. Publicly issued certificates by private financial institutions also provide a cash advance provision, by which the issuer states an intention to advance its own funds to the certificate holder in the event of delinquencies in mortgage loan payments. This cash advance provision, supported by an insurance policy taken out by the issuer, provides for the timely payment of principal and interest on these certificates.

There are essentially five major passthrough security issuers: the GNMA, the Farmers Home Administration (FHmA), the FHLMC, the FNMA, and private financial institutions. As Table 6–6 shows, more than 99 percent of outstanding mortgage passthrough certificates have the implicit guarantee of the three government or quasi-government agencies. Even in their peak

Table 6-6.   Residential Mortgage-Backed Passthrough Certificates Outstanding ($ millions).

Year	GNMA[a]	FHLM[a]	FNMA[a]	FHmA[a]	Private Institutions[b]	Total
1970	347	–	–	2,245	–	2,592
1971	3,074	64	–	3,693	–	6,831
1972	5,504	441	–	5,148	–	11,093
1973	7,890	766	–	5,596	–	14,252
1974	11,769	757	–	6,898	–	19,424
1975	18,257	1,598	–	9,489	–	29,344
1976	30,572	2,671	–	10,751	–	43,994
1977	44,896	6,610	–	12,156	217	63,879
1978	54,347	11,892	–	14,516	878	81,633
1979	76,401	15,182	–	17,047	1,178	109,808
1980	93,874	16,854	–	19,295	1,200	131,223
1981	105,790	19,843	700	21,804	1,200	149,337
1982	118,402	41,278	14,450	24,349	1,200	199,679

[a] Data obtained from the *Federal Reserve Bulletin,* various issues.

[b] Data supplied by Paine, Webber, Jackson, and Curtis, Inc., Corporate Finance Department.

year of 1978 private institutions offered less than 4 percent of new pool certificates issued. In terms of the dollar amount of pools outstanding at the end of 1982, the GNMA accounted for 60 percent of the total, the FHmA 12 percent, the FHLMC 20.5 percent, the FNMA 7.5 percent, and private financial institutions 0.6 percent.

The growth in the aggregate amount of mortgage pool certificates since 1970 is extraordinary. An instrument virtually untried in 1970 today accounts for nearly $200 billion of mortgage debt, more than 20 percent of the single-family home loans outstanding. In 1982 the passthrough certificates added more than $50 billion to the mortgage market.

The initial and still largest source of growth in the mortgage pool securities market is the GNMA. "Any qualified FHA mortgagee who is judged to have adequate experience and facilities to issue mortgage-backed securities and who is approved for a guarantee by GNMA can issue a passthrough security."[8] The issuer services the mortgage for a fee of 0.44 percent, and the GNMA receives a fee of 0.06 percent. In the event of a default by an issuer, the GNMA assumes responsibility for the payments due the certificate holder. The GNMA loan pools are composed primarily of FHA-insured, single-family home mortgages. In the spring of 1979 the GNMA began guaranteeing graduated-payment mortgage loan pools, and by September 1979 these pools accounted for more than 14 percent of the value of new pools issued in that month.

The major issuers of conventional mortgage pools are the FHLMC and FNMA. Unlike the GNMA, the FHLMC directly issues mortgage participation certificates that represent undivided interests in specific pools of mortgages held by the FHLMC. Since 1971 the FHLMC has regularly conducted four separate programs for making commitments to purchase single-family and multifamily conventional mortgages on whole and participatory bases. Mortgage participation certificates were being issued at a $4 billion annual rate from 1974 to 1981. In 1982, because of extensive swapping of pass-through certificates for old mortgages in SLA portfolios, passthrough certificates rose over $20 billion. The FHLMC, which purchases mortgages nearly exclusively from SLAs, serves as the servicer and guarantor of timely payment of interest and principal. Mortgages in FHLMC pools are insured primarily by private mortgage insurance companies. In late 1981 the FNMA also began guaranteeing mortgage passthrough securities; as of the end of 1982 it had guaranteed $14.5 billion worth.

The third source of mortgage passthrough securities is private financial institutions. While they presently represent only slightly more than $1 billion in pools outstanding, they are perceived to have a bright future given the overall size of the conventional mortgage market.[9] Bank of America has issued sixteen of these pools, representing 65 percent of the dollar volume of publicly issued pools by private financial institutions. The only SLA to enter this market in a regular way is Home Savings and Loan Association in Los Angeles.

A final new innovation in the secondary mortgage market in 1983 was the collateralized mortgage obligation (CMO). A CMO is a bond collateralized by mortgages, in which payment streams from the mortgage are segmented into fast, medium, and slow pay divisions. In most of the issues so far payments are semiannual and a minimum repayments timetable has been guaranteed by the issuer. The bond and call protection features are expected to appeal to nontraditional mortgage investors. As of early 1984 over $6 billion worth of CMOs have been issued, half of them by the FHLMC.

It is clear from these figures that agency-guaranteed mortgage passthrough securities have become a major source of mortgage credit in the late 1970s and early 1980s. If we add the net extension of credit by the FNMA and FHLBB, we find that in 1982 the total net volume of activity by these four agencies was nearly $60 billion, or 65 percent of the net mortgage credit extended for one- to four-family housing. Thus, these agencies have become the largest source of mortgage credit—and the key to meeting the mortgage credit gap problem.

This potential solution to the projected mortgage gap in the 1980s has one major constraint. The legislative and executive branches of the federal government are raising serious questions about the policy of guaranteeing such a large volume of mortgages for middle- and upper-income homeowners. These questions are being asked in conjunction with an attempt to limit governmental debt guarantees, especially in cases where there is a vig-orous private sector ready to provide the required services. An argument can be made that these public-backed mortgage certificates reduce the ability of the private sector to compete in this area.

At this point it is not clear whether or not government agencies will be allowed to continue to pursue the guarantor programs they so effectively developed in the past five years. Even if they are not, private passthrough securities with private mortgage insurance are probably a reasonably good substitute. Both the FHLMC and the FNMA are attempting to become fully private institutions. Given the attitude of policymakers and the vital role of this mortgage security type of funding, it would make sense to encourage this privatization of the guarantor function.

Both the countercyclical and the credit supply functions of the federal and quasi-federal agencies will be changing dramatically in the new deregu-lated financial environment. The FNMA and FHLMC are likely to empha-size their private sector guarantor roles and deemphasize their direct coun-tercyclical roles. In the light of present administration policies, the GNMA, in both its countercyclical role and its role as a guarantor, is likely to be sub-stantially reduced. The FHLBB will continue to regulate and provide liquid-ity to a somewhat diminished SLA industry.

THE TRANSITION OF THE HOUSING FINANCE SYSTEM[10]

Over the long haul, deregulation of the deposit market, new sources of mortgage credit, and the wide range of new mortgage instruments (see Chapter 7) will benefit housing and contribute to a more efficient financial system, but the ability of the system to adapt to this new environment in a smooth, nondisruptive manner is questionable. Regulators and financial in-stitutions can avert this potential transition crisis and produce a more effi-cient, equitable, and market-oriented financial system and an adequate, stable flow of funds to the housing industry if they take the right action. To do so they must understand the conditions that bring about the periodic crises in housing. They are:

1. extremely volatile financial market conditions, which create chaos in the fixed-rate debt instrument market;
2. a piecemeal deregulation of financial institutions that has worsened the asset-liability maturity imbalance problem of thrifts and provided nowhere near the flexibility required to meet market needs;
3. a historical experience in which unanticipated inflation has put the entire mortgage portfolio of many institutions "underwater"; and

4. a political attack on housing and housing finance at just the time when the industry is in complete disarray and distress and when an unprecedented number of first-time homebuyers are about to enter the market.

The first problem causing the periodic crises facing the housing finance industry is a direct result of the unprecedented interest rate and monetary instability of the past three years, which must be viewed as a result of unacceptable monetary and fiscal policy: it creates great uncertainty for households and firms and undermines the efficiency of the entire economy. The major cause of this faulty monetary policy is the FRS's failure to anticipate or comprehend some of the key links between its activities and the financial and real sectors of the economy. The major cause of faulty fiscal policy is the Reagan administration's continued support of record federal deficits.

The FRS appears to have erred in several fundamental ways. It seems to have forgotten that FRS policy instruments work with a substantial lag, and so it appears to be reacting to current financial and economic conditions myopically. This myopia has been accentuated by an underestimation of market response to exogenous economic stimuli and FRS activity. While it must clearly focus on a long-run policy of slowing excessive credit growth, the FRS should be sensitive to the violent short-term swings that might accompany its own release of statistically suspect weekly money supply numbers.

Monetary policy does not work through a black box but rather through real and nominal interest rates. Real interest rates are the ultimate determinant of investment and economic activity. Nominal interest rates are also of major importance in certain sectors of the economy, such as housing. FRS policy led to violent fluctuations in both the real and financial sectors of the economy in 1980, 1981, and 1982, impairing efficiency in the real sector and thus ultimately raising the cost of production. As a result, short-run, anti-inflationary, destabilizing actions of the FRS have actually contributed to long-run inflation.

A second problem confronting thrift institutions is the piecemeal deregulation of the industry. On the liability side, two deposit maturities have been deregulated. Failure, until 1983, to introduce medium- and long-term accounts with market rates has shortened the average life of deposit liabilities and greatly worsened the asset-liability maturity imbalance faced by SLAs.

On the asset side there was only a minimal amount of deregulation until the spring of 1981. The prior range of mortgage instruments was far too inflexible to allow SLAs to support their volatile short-term deposit structure. Policymakers responsible for deregulation clearly should have proceeded on asset-side flexibility prior to, or at least coincident with, liability-side flexibility. Their failure to do so shows an insensitivity to the transition problem faced by thrift institutions.

The third condition relates to this asset-liability imbalance and the unanticipated inflation of the past ten years, which has forced thrift institutions to pay market rates on more than 75 percent of their liabilities and yet maintain a portfolio of old mortgages—those made prior to the 1981 deregulation—far below current market interest rates. The result is a situation in which thrifts have an unrealized portfolio loss of more than $100 billion. In addition, because market rates on deposit liabilities have risen dramatically while asset yields have risen only modestly, most thrifts experienced a very negative earnings situation in 1980–82. Even in 1983 earnings were positive only because of nonrecurring gains and purchase accounting. There has been a massive erosion of net worth, which bodes poorly for the viability of thrifts during the next interest rate cycle. Overregulation of the thrift industry is largely to blame for this situation.

The final feature of this crisis was the unprecedented political attack on the housing industry and the specialized housing finance system. At a time when housing construction was as its lowest level in three decades and the thrift industry was barely surviving, it was extremely poor public policy to undermine further an already weak system. While there may have been past excesses in the construction and financing industries, in 1980–1982 housing did not receive an adequate share of financial or real resources.

By early summer 1981 the transition crisis was becoming increasingly apparent to federal regulators and public policy officials. By the second quarter of 1981 it was estimated that over 90 percent of thrift institutions were losing money and that over 300 might exhaust their net worth by year end. In the search for a mechanism to avert a complete collapse of the regulated thrift industry the "all-savers certificate" (ASC) was included in the tax bill signed in August 1981. The ASC was a one-year certificate of deposit with the interest on the deposit tax free up to a maximum of $1,000 for a single person and $2,000 for a married couple. Only regulated financial institutions could offer this certificate, thus excluding competition from money market mutual funds. The interest rate of the ASC was pegged to 70 percent of the latest "investment yield" on the most recent one-year Treasury note auction. The rate was fixed for the one-year holding period of the note, early withdrawal resulting in a loss of tax exemption.

The ASC was first issued on October 1, 1981, and was last issued in December 1982. The initial tax-free interest rate offered October 1 was 12.61 percent. A deposit of $15,872 was thus required for a married couple wanting to earn the maximum allowed tax-free interest.

One final provision of the ASC legislation was that 75 percent of the net new money attracted to these accounts was to be invested in housing or agricultural loans and was intended to provide transition assistance for the buyers, builders, and sellers of homes.

The cost of this transition program was substantial. With the $53 billion of assets deposited in ASCs, the government lost nearly $2 billion of tax revenues. Since this program was targeted not only at thrifts, estimates are that only 43 percent of this forgone tax revenue went to reduce thrift institution losses. The rest of the reduction was dispersed among CBs and credit unions, with perhaps a small amount of additional benefits accruing to the consumers and suppliers of housing.

This partial "reregulation" of the deposit market was a costly and inefficient mechanism for smoothing out the transition problem. A far better approach would have been to induce a moderate decline in interest rates and institute a complete immediate deregulation of the deposit markets, which would have allowed the thrifts an opportunity to extend the maturity on their deposit liabilities and to move quickly toward a restructuring of their asset side, using the more flexible mortgage instruments now available. The FRS's monetary policy, which produced record high real interest rates, vastly exacerbated the transition problem. The result was the ASC, which was itself deficit-creating and counterproductive to FRS goals. The FRS could have quite consistently let short-term Treasury bill rates fall to the 10 percent level, still allowing a nominal 1 to 2 percent real rate, and reduce the transition problem for the housing finance system.

Not until fall 1982 did the FRB follow this advice. With the fall of Treasury bill rates to the 8 to 9 percent level and the full deregulation of deposits with the introduction of MMDAs, the transition problem facing the housing finance system has been temporarily averted. The challenge of the mid-1980s is to force the regulators to handle this sensitive transition process from a highly regulated financial environment to a market-oriented financial system in a cost efficient manner. If the FRS continues to rely solely on a monetary aggregates policy and makes no plans to achieve an orderly structural consolidation of the regulated financial system, in all likelihood a large federal bailout will be necessary. The large current and prospective federal budget deficits and the rising interest rates they have engendered in the first half of 1984 make a federal bailout inevitable.

NOTES

1. For a more extended analysis see Kenneth Rosen and James Kearl, *A Model of Housing Starts, Mortgage Flows, and the Behavior of the Federal Home Loan Bank Board and the Federal National Mortgage Association,* Paper no. 27, Joint Center for Urban Studies, MIT–Harvard, June 1974; Dwight Jaffee and Kenneth Rosen, "Estimates of the Effectiveness of Stabilization Policies for the Mortgage and Housing Markets," *Journal of Finance* (June 1978); Kenneth Rosen and David Bloom, "A Micro-Economic Model of Federal Home Loan Mortgage Corporation Activity,"

Journal of Finance (September 1980); Kenneth Rosen, "The Federal National Mortgage Association, Residential Construction and Mortgage Lending," Paper 80-12, Center for Real Estate and Urban Economics, University of California, Berkeley, 1980; Dwight Jaffee and Kenneth Rosen, "Mortgage Credit Availability and Residential Construction," *Brookings Papers on Economic Activity* (1979).

2. For more details on the actual model used for the evaluation and for the results of the simulations, see Rosen and Kearl, *A Model of Housing Starts*; and Jaffee and Rosen, "Estimates of the Effectiveness of Stabilization Policies."

3. Rosen, "The Federal National Mortgage Association."

4. Rosen and Bloom, "Micro-Economic Model of Federal Home Loan Mortgage Corporation Activity."

5. For a detailed analysis, see the General Accounting Office (GAO) report on the GNMA emergency housing program. GAO, *What Was the Effect of the Emergency Housing Program on Single-Family Housing Construction?* (Washington, D.C.: Government Printing Office).

6. This analysis comes from Jaffee and Rosen, "Estimates of the Effectiveness of Stabilization Policies."

7. The following sections are derived from Rosen, "The Use of Mortgage Pass-through Securities," in *Proceedings of the Fifth Annual Conference on New Sources of Capital for the Savings and Loan Industry* (Federal Home Loan Bank of San Francisco, 1979), pp. 129–59.

8. Richard G. Marcis, "Mortgage-Backed Securities: Their Uses and Potential for Broadening the Sources of Mortgage Credit," *Journal of Economics and Business* (Winter 1975).

9. Richard G. Marcis, "Mortgage-Backed Securities: Financial Alternatives for Savings and Loan Associations," FHLBB *Journal,* November 1978.

10. This portion of the chapter is adapted from a presentation at the December 1980 Sixth Annual Conference of the Federal Home Loan Bank of San Francisco, which appears in *Proceedings of the Sixth Annual Conference on Savings and Loan Asset Management Under Deregulation* (1980).

Chapter 7

Making Housing Affordable:
New Mortgage Instruments

Today, less than one-third of American families can afford the median-priced, single-family house. Housing analysts, including this author, have a long tradition of declaring housing crises when a large number of those who are seeking housing cannot afford it. In the 1960s the cost of credit appeared to create major problems; in the 1970s the rising price of houses was the prime villain; in the early 1980s a combination of high prices and record high interest rates were the culprits. At the period of peak mortgage rates in 1981 only 7 percent of families could afford the median-priced home according to some estimates. The collapse of the single-family home market from 1980 to 1982 provides some evidence confirming these alarmist views.

There were also positive developments. The majority of households that owned homes made huge capital gains on their housing investment in the 1970s, and the majority of renters saw their real rent decline substantially during that period. Clearly, there is a need for careful interpretation of the affordability questions before a crisis can be declared and policies formulated.

MEASURES OF AFFORDABILITY

In order to analyze the issue of housing affordability, it is necessary to divide those who use housing into four categories: (1) renters, (2) first-time purchasers, (3) households moving from an owned housing unit into another such unit, and (4) households occupying housing they own and do not plan to leave. These categories of households experienced very different cost trends in the 1970s that are likely to persist into the mid-1980s.

How affordability is measured is also critical to an understanding of the issue. The traditional measure has been a ratio of current housing expenses to current income. The accepted norm has been that households should not spend more than 25 to 30 percent of their incomes on housing. This criterion may have been appropriate during periods of stable and low inflation, but recent economic conditions may require a different standard.

An increasingly popular alternative among economists and, judging from market behavior, consumers emphasizes the investment aspect of housing. This perspective, which looks at the cost of homeowning after tax advantages and expected property appreciation are explicitly considered, applies mainly to homeowning. This cost is then compared with current income, expected income, or both.

The key to assessing the affordability problem is to identify the appropriate affordability measure for each consumer type. More detailed consideration of these measures is warranted.

Current Costs — Current Income Concepts

First-time Homebuyers.   When purchasing a first home a household faces current interest rates, current house prices, and payments for property taxes and utilities. In order to measure the cash costs the first-time homebuyer faces over time, each of these costs must be estimated.

Although it has been heavily criticized because of its high weighting on current mortgage interest rates, the homeownership component of the consumer price index (CPI) is a good composite measure of these costs for first-time homebuyers. Table 7-1 shows the composite index and various components of the index over the 1970s. This table also depicts the annual payments — including mortgage payments, property taxes (1.5% of sale price), maintenance, repair, and insurance (1%) — on the median-priced existing home. The table also shows data on the other financial hurdles to the first-time buyer: median down payment requirement on the median-priced existing single-family home. Median household income is included as a measure of current cash flows.

These data show a startling deterioration in housing affordability as measured by the payment-income ratio since the mid-1970s. In the early 1970s the 20 to 25 percent income ratio looked quite reasonable. By 1978 the ratio had risen by nearly ten percentage points. Since mortgage interest rates were virtually unchanged, this was due almost exclusively to the rise in house prices. In 1980–82 unprecedented levels of mortgage interest rates raised the payment-income ratio to 45 percent, nearly double the level of the early 1970s.

Table 7-1. Housing Costs.

Year	Home-ownership Component CPI (1)	Median Sales Price, New Home ($) (2)	Median Sales Price, Existing Home ($) (3)	Effective Mortgage Interest Rate (%) (4)	Median Down Payment, Existing Home ($) (5)	Annual Payments, Existing Home ($) (6)	Median Annual Household Income ($) (7)	Annual Payment-Income Ratio (6)/(7) ×100 (8)
1970	128.5	23,400	23,000	8.45	6,647	1,957	8,734	22.4
1971	133.7	25,200	24,800	7.74	6,473	2,038	9,028	22.6
1972	140.1	27,600	26,700	7.60	6,408	2,210	9,697	22.8
1973	146.7	32,500	28,900	7.95	7,168	2,450	10,512	23.3
1974	163.2	35,900	32,000	8.92	8,832	2,867	11,101	25.8
1975	181.7	39,300	35,300	9.01	9,389	3,217	11,197	28.7
1976	191.7	44,200	38,100	8.99	9,982	3,480	12,686	27.4
1977	204.9	48,800	42,900	9.01	10,682	3,975	13,572	29.3
1978	227.2	55,700	48,700	9.54	12,126	4,707	15,064	31.2
1979	262.4	62,900	55,700	10.77	14,482	5,832	16,461	35.4
1980	314.0	64,600	62,200	12.66	16,507	7,340	17,710	41.4
1981	352.7	68,900	66,400	14.70	18,007	8,774	19,074	46.0
1982	376.8	69,280	67,800	15.12	19,069	9,063	19,970	45.4

Source: *Federal Reserve Bulletin, Federal Home Loan Bank Board Journal,* Bureau of the Census, National Association of Realtors.

Another way of expressing the affordability crisis facing first-time home-buyers is to determine the income required to support an 80 percent mortgage on the median-priced house assuming the household pays only 30 percent of its income for the housing costs. In 1970 over 60 percent of households qualified for a mortgage on the median-priced home. While the sharp fall in interest rates in 1983 improved affordability, fully two-thirds of households still do not qualify for a mortgage on a median-priced home. These numbers, although less dramatic than those reported in the popular press, show a substantial deterioration in affordability. At the same time, they are misleading because they ignore some of the positive effects that inflation has on the potential first-time homebuyer: inflation also raises homebuyers' expected nominal income and capital gains from homeownership.

The mortgage interest rate is directly affected by the rate of inflation. It is determined by adding the expected inflation rate to a real interest. High inflation rates have raised the contract interest rate, raising the monthly carrying costs of a conventional mortgage by over 60 percent in recent years. The present monthly carrying costs of a conventional mortgage are over four times higher than would be expected given a 1 to 2 percent rate of inflation. This rise in mortgage payments, and the corresponding rise in the initial yearly payments-income ratio, is the genesis of the affordability crisis.

In fact, high nominal mortgage rates have not created the crisis. Rather, high mortgage rates juxtaposed with the archaic institutional mechanisms of the mortgage market have created the problem. If the institutional arrangements of the mortgage market were more flexible there would be no affordability problem as long as real mortgage rates were stable.

The institutional arrangements that prevail in today's mortgage market were established for a low-inflation world. The standard mortgage instrument is basically a level-payment, amortized loan. This loan is not well adapted to an inflationary environment. From the borrower's viewpoint the standard mortgage instrument completely ignores the positive, inflation-induced characteristics of the housing market. In an inflationary environment it makes no sense to use a loan qualification criterion based on an inflation-bloated interest rate but a noninflated income. From the lender's perspective the standard mortgage instrument does attempt, even though very imperfectly, to anticipate the influence of an inflationary environment on the contract. The mortgage interest rate incorporates lender expectations of inflation over the life of the loan. In the past decades, lenders, like the rest of society, have vastly underestimated the rate of inflation. The failure of the standard mortgage instrument and mortgage-qualifying criteria to adapt to an inflationary environment has created a dynamic mismatch between the cost of the mortgage loan and the ability of the borrower to pay. These archaic institutions are a major part of the housing crisis.

The extent of this mismatch can best be illustrated by a simple set of examples. For this example we assume that a household with an income of $20,000 takes out a $50,000, 8.5 percent, twenty-five-year mortgage. Further, assume that the economy experiences 5 percent annual average inflation over the life of the mortgage and that the household experiences a 2 percent real income growth per year. As a second case raise the inflation assumption to 10 percent and the mortgage rate to 13.5 percent. In a third case raise the inflation assumption to 15 percent and the mortgage rate to 18.5 percent. In a final case assume no inflation and a 3.5 percent mortgage rate. Table 7–2 and Figure 7–1 show the dynamic payment streams in the 15 percent, 10 percent, 5 percent, and no-inflation world.

Table 7–2.   Impact of Inflation on the Mortgage Instrument.

Year (1)	Annual Nominal Payment (2)	Annual Real Payment (3)	Annual Nominal Income (4)	Payment Income (2)/(4)
No-Inflation World, $50,000 Mortgage, 3½% Interest Rate				
1	2119.91	2119.91	20,000	10.60
5	2119.91	2119.91	22,082	9.60
10	2119.91	2119.91	24,380	8.70
15	2119.91	2119.91	26,917	7.88
20	2119.91	2119.91	29,719	7.13
25	2119.91	2119.91	32,812	6.46
5% Inflation World, $50,000 Mortgage, 8½% Interest Rate				
1	4831.38	4831.38	20,000	24.16
5	4831.38	3551.50	28,050	17.22
10	4831.38	2748.08	39,342	12.28
15	4831.38	2126.41	55,179	8.75
20	4831.38	1645.38	82,808	5.83
25	4831.38	1273.16	116,142	4.16
10% Inflation World, $50,000 Mortgage, 13½% Interest Rate				
1	6993.86	6993.86	20,000	34.97
5	6993.86	4342.63	35,247	19.84
10	6993.86	2696.43	62,117	11.26
15	6993.86	1674.27	109,471	6.39
20	6993.86	1039.59	192,926	3.62
25	6993.86	645.51	340,000	2.06
15% Inflation World, $50,000 Mortgage, 18½% Interest Rate				
1	9345	9345	20,000	46.72
5	9345	4646.11	43,849	21.31
10	9345	2309.94	96,137	9.72
15	9345	1148.45	210,774	4.43
20	9345	570.98	462,111	2.02
25	9345	283.88	1,013,156	.92

Source: Author's calculations.

Figure 7-1. Payment to Income Ratios over Mortgage Term.

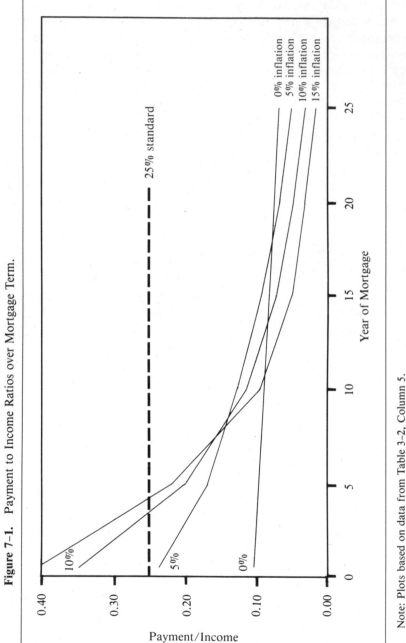

Note: Plots based on data from Table 3–2, Column 5.
Assumes: 3½% real mortgage rate; $50,000 mortgage; beginning income of $20,000; real income growth of 2%; nominal income growth of 2% + inflation; nominal mortgage rate of 3½% + inflation.

It is clear from these comparative examples that even a moderate inflation rate induces a major distortion in the time path of payments relative to income. A 5 percent inflation rate more than doubles the initial payment-income ratio compared to the no-inflation world. By the tenth year the household in the 5 percent world with an 8.5 percent mortgage is paying only 12 percent of its income to amortize the mortgage; by the last year of the mortgage it is paying only 4.2 percent of income for the mortgage. Real payments would have dropped from $4,831 per year to only $1,273 per year by the fiscal year of the mortgage.

In the high-inflation cases of 10 percent and 15 percent with mortgage rates at 13.5 percent and 18.5 percent respectively, the distortion is so large as to make the results ludicrous. In the 15 percent inflation world the nominal payment-income ratio is nearly 50 percent in the initial year, five times the payments in the no-inflation world. By the fifth year the payment-income ratio would have dropped to a reasonable 20 percent and by the tenth year to less than 10 percent. By the twenty-fifth year the payments are less than 1 percent of the household's "modest" $1 million income.

To summarize, the first-time homebuyer in a high-inflation world with our archaic mortgage instrument and qualifying criteria based on a first-year payment-income ratio does indeed face an affordability crisis. One could contend, however, that as long as the intrinsic real rate of interest has not changed, the affordability crisis is in fact a phony artifact of a lending system that is inappropriate for an inflationary environment.

Existing Homeowners.   Households that already own their own homes are in a far different affordability situation than first-time homebuyers. Housing analysts (including this author) have derived much publicity from the statement that only a small portion of present homeowners could afford to buy their present house at current interest rates and current prices. While this is true, present homeowners in fact do not have to face current interest rates and prices. If they are nonmovers they face historic interest rates and historic prices which are fixed at the time of purchase, while at the same time their nominal income is presumably rising. Thus, nonmovers who have purchased homes in the past are in that portion of the curve (shown in Figure 7-1) where their house payment-income ratio is falling. In a cash flow sense their real cost of housing is declining, assuming that property taxes and utility and maintenance costs are not rising too rapidly. In an opportunity cost sense, however, their cost of housing is not declining as rapidly. While the mortgage payments are fixed at historic values, because of the rising value of their house, the implicit rental on the equity component of the housing expenditure is rising. This represents the return that could be earned if the equity funds invested in the house were invested elsewhere. As a result, one must combine the fixed mortgage payments with the rising implicit rental cost of housing equity to arrive at an overall opportunity cost of home-owning.

Existing homeowners who decide to move face a cash payment-income problem similar to first-time homebuyers in that they are forced to pay current prices and mortgage rates. This can be an especially severe problem if they move from a low-cost housing area to a high-cost housing area or move during a period of cyclical tightness in the market. Offsetting this current price-income squeeze on homeowner-movers is the large capital gain they have probably made on their previous home. They can directly use this capital gain to reduce monthly payments on the newly purchased home by putting up a larger down payment. Alternatively, they could invest the equity from the capital gain and use the income to offset the higher monthly payments. While homeowner-movers can take full advantage of this equity accumulation, unless their mortgages are assumable they cannot capitalize the value of their low-interest, fixed-rate mortgages. If the old mortgage can be assumed by the new owner, the previous owner can command a higher price for the property.

Existing homeowners, whether movers or nonmovers, do not in general face an affordability problem. In fact, the cost of owner-occupied housing over the past decade has been dramatically reduced for this group when property appreciation is part of the calculation.

Renters.   Analyzing the current payment-current income ratio of renters is straightforward. Comparison of median rents with median household income over the past decade shows a declining payment-income ratio. Table 7–3 shows that this payment-income ratio had a slight downtrend since the early 1970s, with the ratio dropping to 14.8 percent in 1980 and rising to 15.4 percent in 1982. These numbers understate the affordability problem of renters, as the all-household income figures overstate the income of renters. Table 7–3, which also shows the income of renters and the rent-renter income ratio for selected years, reveals a higher rent-income number but with a trend that is slightly down through 1981. From the available numbers there does not appear to be an aggregate affordability problem in the rental segment of the housing market.

After-Tax Capital Cost of Homeownership

An increasingly popular measure of the cost of homeownership is an index that incorporates the current cash costs of homeownership, the opportunity cost of the implicit rental on the owner's equity, the tax benefits from owning, and the expected capital gains of the owners. This measure of home-ownership is far more representative of the affordability of homeownership

Table 7-3.   Rental Costs, 1970–1982.

Year	Rental Component CPI	Median Rent[a] (annual) ($)	Rent/All-Household Income (%)	Income of Renters ($)	Rent/ Renter Income (%)
1970	110.1	1,446	16.6	6,300	22.9
1971	115.2	1,513	16.8		
1972	119.2	1,565	16.1		
1973	124.3	1,633	15.5		
1974	130.6	1,716	15.5	7,700	22.9
1975	137.3	1,804	16.1		
1976	114.7	2,004	15.8	8,100	24.7
1977	153.5	2,116	15.6		
1978	164.0	2,254	15.0	9,300	24.2
1979	176.0	2,412	14.7		
1980	191.6	2,626	14.8		
1981	208.2	2,853	15.0	13,245	21.5
1982	224.0	3,070	15.4		

[a] Calculated using *Annual Housing Survey* and Bureau of Labor Statistics rental CPI component.

Source: *Annual Housing Survey*; Bureau of the Census; Bureau of Labor Statistics; and author's calculations.

than is the current cost-current income measure. Table 7–4 shows each of the major components of this measure for the 1970s as they would be perceived by a potential homebuyer in any particular year.

The trends in mortgage interest costs, if considered by themselves, have reduced the ability of households to buy homes. This negative impact of inflation on interest is balanced by increased tax benefits because of the deductibility of nominal mortgage interest payments and property taxes. Tax benefits have risen because of the sharp rise in mortgage interest payments and the inflation-induced marginal tax bracket creep of the median-income family household. On the other hand, the benefit to itemizing deductions has been reduced by a substantial real increase in the standard deduction.

While the tax benefits due to owning a home have increased only moderately, the expected capital gains benefit of owning has increased dramatically, reflecting accelerating economywide inflation as well as specific housing market conditions. In fact, until 1981 the expected capital gains benefit had been so high as to balance many of the other costs of ownership. Figure 7–2 shows the real percent change in house prices in the last fifteen years. If financial institutions used the capital cost of ownership as their loan-qualifying criterion then the affordability crisis would not have existed, at least

Table 7-4. Capital Cost of Housing for the Median-Priced Existing Home, 1970–1982.

Year	Mortgage Interest Payments ($)	Opportunity Cost of Equity[a] ($)	Maintenance Repair, Property Taxes, Depreciation[b] ($)	Tax Benefits[c] ($)	Expected Capital Gains[d] ($)	Total Capital Cost ($)	Total Capital Costs/House-hold Income (%)
1970	1,381	562	575	296	1,244	978	11.2
1971	1,418	501	620	292	1,567	681	7.5
1972	1,542	487	668	299	1,633	764	7.9
1973	1,728	570	723	307	1,966	746	7.1
1974	2,066	788	800	364	2,400	891	8.0
1975	2,335	846	882	407	2,867	789	7.1
1976	2,528	893	953	421	3,067	891	7.0
1977	2,903	963	1,072	474	3,633	830	6.1
1978	3,489	1,157	1,218	573	4,467	823	5.5
1979	4,439	1,560	1,392	754	5,867	771	4.7
1980	5,785	2,090	1,555	1,041	6,433	1,955	11.0
1981	7,114	2,647	1,660	1,295	5,900	4,225	22.2
1982	7,368	2,883	1,695	1,315	4,033	6,598	33.0

[a] Uses the mortgage rate as the opportunity costs interest rate.

[b] 2.5 percent of purchase price.

[c] Utilizes a 25 percent marginal tax rate and a 5.4 standard deduction to calculate tax benefits from itemizing mortgage interest and property tax deduction.

[d] A three-year moving average of actual capital gains.

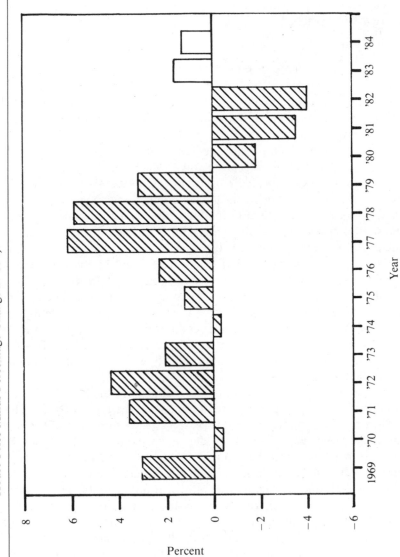

Figure 7-2. Real Median Existing House Price Change (Percentage Change Median Existing House Price Minus Percentage Change in CPI).

until 1980. The behavior of households indicates that they were fully aware that the capital cost rather than the current cost was the appropriate decisionmaking variable. Beginning in 1981 and continuing through most of 1982, high real interest rates and declining real house prices raised the cost of capital to unprecedented levels. Thus, in those years both capital and current costs reached unaffordable levels.

Affordability in the mid-1980s

Using the most common measure of affordability—current payment divided by current income—the outlook for the mid-1980s is somewhat improved. Even if inflation rates of the past several years do not stay at the 3 to 5 percent range of 1983 but average 6 percent, nominal mortgage rates are still likely to stay in the 11 to 14 percent range, which sets the minimum payment-income ratio, given expected housing prices, in the 35 to 40 percent range. This is relatively good news, as at least nominal mortgage rates will not rise further to exacerbate the affordability problem. However, the high real interest rates create a continuing affordability problem for households though the problem is less severe than in the early 1980s. Given a 6 percent overall inflation rate house prices will rise between 6.3 and 7 percent per year, while median household income is expected to rise at a 7.9 percent rate. The result would be a decreasing income-price gap over the decade. The net effect of high but declining mortgage interest rates and rising relative house prices is that the median payment-median income ratio, which rose to 45 percent in 1982, will decline to about 35 percent in 1992. (See Table 7–5.) Based on the current payment-income ratio, affordability will be increased somewhat in the mid- and late 1980s.

A continuing negative factor in affordability for the 1980s is the expected continued high down payment requirement on the typical house. This continuing high median loan-to-value ratio is in part a product of the emerging mortgage credit gap. The strong demand for housing and rising relative house prices create a strong demand for mortgage credit. At the same time, high inflation rates and a tax system that discourages savings and investment have produced a lag in the supply of funds available for loans. One of the consequences of this gap will be adjustment of mortgage rate terms to bring the supply and demand for credit into balance. Relative mortgage rates and median loan-to-value ratios will remain high in the 1980s.

The capital cost measure of housing affordability shows an even more favorable trend (see Table 7–6). The tax benefit component will become substantially more important because of the rise in nominal interest rates relative to the 1970s. (This assumes that the excess standard deduction remains at 5.4 percent of median household incomes and that the marginal

Table 7-5. Housing Costs in the 1980s.

Year	Home-ownership Component CPI (1)	Median Sales Price, New Home ($) (2)	Median Sales Price, Existing Home ($) (3)	Effective Mortgage Interest Rate (%) (4)	Median Down Payment, Existing Home (%) (5)	Annual Payments, Existing Home ($) (6)	Median Annual Household Income ($) (7)	Annual Payment-Income Ratio (6)/(7)×100 (8)
1983	393.3	76,446	70,498	13.1	19,404	8,457	21,148	40.0
1984	415.4	81,536	74,583	12.6	19,598	8,772	22,650	38.7
1985	434.3	87,649	79,445	12.5	21,204	9,251	24,372	38.0
1986	462.8	94,539	85,217	12.6	22,805	10,021	26,248	38.2
1987	492.2	99,113	89,782	12.8	24,481	10,629	27,849	38.2
1988	514.0	104,378	94,783	12.5	26,097	10,968	29,660	37.0
1989	540.4	111,937	101,246	12.6	28,023	11,730	32,032	36.6
1990	569.4	122,976	110,730	12.2	30,533	12,536	34,531	36.3
1991	602.4	129,857	117,082	12.2	32,543	12,223	37,051	35.7
1992	624.0	138,055	124,823	11.8	34,012	13,831	40,015	34.6

Table 7-6. Capital Cost of Housing for the Median-Priced Existing Home, 1983–1992.

Year	Mortgage Interest Payments ($)	Opportunity Cost of Equity[a] ($)	Maintenance, Repair, Property Taxes, Depreciation[b] ($)	Tax Benefits[c] ($)	Expected Capital Gains[d] ($)	Total Capital Cost ($)	Total Capital Costs/Household Income (%)
1983	6,694	2,542	1,762	1,092	2,766	7,141	33.8
1984	6,907	2,462	1,864	1,078	2,727	7,428	32.8
1985	7,264	2,645	1,986	1,091	3,881	6,923	28.4
1986	7,890	2,883	2,130	1,166	4,906	6,832	26.0
1987	8,384	3,143	2,244	1,218	5,066	7,487	26.9
1988	8,598	3,267	2,369	1,191	5,112	7,930	26.7
1989	9,199	3,520	2,531	1,235	5,343	8,672	27.1
1990	9,757	3,714	2,768	1,273	6,982	7,984	23.1
1991	10,296	3,963	2,927	1,292	7,432	8,461	22.8
1992	10,710	4,011	3,120	1,261	7,858	8,722	21.3

[a] Uses the mortgage rate as the opportunity costs interest rate.

[b] 2.5 percent of purchase price.

[c] Utilizes a 25 percent marginal tax rate and a 5.4 standard deduction to calculate tax benefits from itemizing mortgage interest and property tax deduction.

[d] A three-year moving average of actual capital gains.

Table 7-7. Rental Costs in the 1980s.

Year	Rental Component CPI	Median Rent (annual) ($)	Rent/All-Household Income (%)
1983	233.0	3,194	15.1
1984	245.5	3,364	14.9
1985	260.8	3,574	14.7
1986	280.5	3,844	14.6
1987	302.5	4,145	14.9
1988	323.8	4,438	15.0
1989	347.1	4,756	14.8
1990	375.2	5,142	14.9
1991	405.3	5,554	15.0
1992	436.1	5,976	14.9

tax rate of the median household remains at 25 percent.) Moreover, the rising relative price of housing means that the expected capital gains component of the cost of homeownership continues nearly to outweigh the mortgage interest and opportunity cost of homeowning. The net effect is that the capital cost-income ratio is at a higher level than in the early 1980s but declines by over one-third in the decade. By this measure homeownership is also becoming somewhat more affordable in the mid-1980s.

The final measure of housing costs, the rent-income ratio, shows continued stability, with the rent-income ratio remaining in the 15 percent range (22 percent for renters), and suggests that there will be no rental affordability problem in the 1980s, even though real rents will rise faster in the 1980s than in the previous decade. (See Table 7-7.)

To summarize, using the conventional measure of affordability, current payment-current income, the late 1970s and the early 1980s showed an affordability crisis for first-time homebuyers. Using the capital cost of housing measure showed that housing was more affordable if only the household can overcome the initial entry barriers erected by the fixed-payment mortgage and down payment requirements. As we move through the 1980s housing will become somewhat more affordable. However, the challenge of the 1980s is to devise an institutional structure that will allow the first-time homebuyer to purchase the home he or she certainly can afford by any investment criteria.

DEREGULATED MORTGAGE INSTRUMENTS

In the spring of 1981 major changes were authorized in the types of mortgage instruments offered by federally chartered financial institutions. In

March 1981 the comptroller of the currency allowed national banks to make an adjustable-rate mortgage (ARM) loan. Interest rates could be raised or lowered, according to changes in a specified index, by 1 percent every six months. There was no limit on the cumulative change in the interest rates over the life of the loan. In April 1981 the chairman of the Federal Home Loan Bank Board (FHLBB) far exceeded the comptroller's efforts and completely deregulated the mortgage instrument. The adjustable-mortgage loan (AML) was authorized, under which no limits were placed on payments or interest rate adjustments on a periodic or cumulative basis. Any index readily verifiable by consumers and beyond the control of lenders could be used for interest rate or payment adjustments.

In March 1983, the comptroller of the currency issued new regulations for national banks allowing them to use any interest rate index upon which to base their adjustable-rate mortgage indices. These new ARM regulations also removed all limits on periodic or aggregate changes to interest rates or monthly payment amounts. In July 1981 the FHLBB also authorized a combined graduated-payment mortgage (GPM) and AML with no limit on negative amortization.[1]

These changes in federal regulations are bringing forth a revolution in the housing finance system. They have been quickly reflected in changes in state laws granting parity to state-chartered institutions.

The fixed-payment fixed-interest-rate mortgage (FPM) has been the mainstay of the housing finance system for nearly thirty years. In the present environment of volatile, high interest and inflation rates, this instrument has created a serious profitability crisis for lenders and an affordability crisis for homebuyers. In this economic environment the FPM serves neither the borrower nor lender well.

The changes in federal regulation of deposit interest rates described earlier have been a major impetus for change. The new federal regulations mean that the 1980s will be a decade in which depository institutions will be forced to compete for liabilities in a deregulated environment. The introduction of the money market deposit account (MMDA) and other variable-rate certificates means that the financial institutions have to pay market rates for nearly all short- and intermediate-term liabilities. It is quite likely that SLAs and commercial banks (CBs) will be completely deregulated for the full spectrum of maturities in the near future.

While deposit rate flexibility on all maturity classes would go a long way toward ensuring a competitive deposit market, the ability of financial institutions to pay market returns on liabilities without causing massive failures may be a problem. They can only do this if they are also allowed to receive market rates on their assets. The movement toward market rates on liabilities has required regulators to introduce new mortgage instruments that will allow mortgage providers to receive market rates on their assets.

Description of New Mortgage Loan Instruments

There are four major classes of new mortgage loans that will be used in the mortgage market of the 1980s. The first type is the variable-rate mortgage (VRM). This category includes the AML, the ARM, the roll over mortgage, and the renegotiable-rate mortgage. In each of these instruments the mortgage interest rate can be adjusted when there is sufficient movement of a market-based index. The second type (actually first authorized on a limited basis in 1977) is the GPM. Payments in the early years of a GPM loan are substantially lower than those necessary to amortize the loan, but they rise gradually at a preset rate for a number of years. The third type is the shared-appreciation mortgage (SAM). While not yet authorized for use by regulated financial institutions, SAMs are in limited use in the private market. The final class of mortgages combines aspects of the variable-rate and graduated-payment loans. It is best described as a dual-interest-rate mortgage (DIM), for the borrower faces different interest rates for payment and amortization purposes.

Variable-Rate Mortgage.   Initially the new federal regulations created two types of VRMs. The comptroller's regulations, which applied to national banks, created an ARM. This type of loan allowed the interest rate to be adjusted by 1 percent every six months. These rate adjustments were tied to one of three indices: the FHLBB's national mortgage rate closing index, the three-year Treasury securities rate, or the six-month Treasury bill rate. If the rate change calculated by the change in the relevant index rate exceeded the 1 percent per six months cap, the excess could be carried over and used in the next adjustment period. There was no cumulative restraint on the interest rate adjustment although the six-month cap implied a 59 percent increase limit for a thirty-year mortgage. A number of banks imposed a 3 to 5 percent overall cap on interest rate increases as a result of market pressures. The only legal restriction on payment changes came indirectly, through the limitation on accumulated negative amortization. Negative amortization was permitted under the ARM regulations as long as it did not exceed 10 percent of the principal loan balance at the beginning of any five-year period. A substantial interest rate rise could have induced a payment increase to avoid violating the negative amortization constraint.

The AML, authorized by the FHLBB, was far more liberal. It provided virtually complete flexibility for the thrift institutions in designing a mortgage instrument. There were essentially no periodic or cumulative ceilings on interest rate or payment adjustments and no restrictions on the accumulation of negative amortization. The only requirement was that the index used for rate adjustment be readily verifiable by the borrower and free of control by the lender. Any of the comptroller-suggested indices were acceptable, as were a wide range of market rates, including the FHLBB cost of funds index. A popular alternative to the semiannual payment adjustment mechanism was the use of a fixed-payment instrument for three to five years, followed by a full payment adjustment. In March 1983 the comptroller of the currency made the ARM conform with the more flexible AML regulations.

In allowing so much flexibility the FHLBB showed great confidence that market competition would force prudent and efficient limitations on the mortgage instrument. From both the lender's and borrower's viewpoint some form of payment cap seems essential. To reduce the risk of default the lender would want to limit payment changes to some reasonable amount. The borrower also would want to limit payment changes so that they approximate expected income changes. Market pressures have led to widespread acceptance of a 7.5 percent annual cap on payment increases and a 3 to 5 percent cumulative cap on mortgage interest rate increases. There are, however, some institutions offering mortgage instruments in which payment increases are likely to be 20 to 30 percent within a year even without an interest rate change. These types of instruments clearly violate normal ethical business practice if not fully disclosed to the consumer.

Any of these capped or fixed-payment instruments could be subject to substantial negative amortization. This makes lenders, secondary-market purchasers, and private mortgage insurers want to limit the loan-to-current market value ratio to something less than 100 percent. In extremely unusual circumstances, the loan-to-current value ratio cap and the annual payment cap could come into conflict, causing either a very large payment increase or a potential default on the property. This outcome is highly unlikely under most economic scenarios and any reasonable set of initial pricing schemes. In early 1984, however, overly aggressive initial pricing schemes threaten to produce a substantially higher incidence of payment and collateral shock.

Graduated-Payment Mortgage.   The crux of the borrower's problem is the high (relative to income) payments in the early years of the mortgage loan due to the inflation premium in the mortgage interest rate. The obvious solution to this problem is a GPM. The GPM reduces payments in the early years of the mortgage while allowing gradually increasing payments over time. In contrast to the VRM, the contract mortgage rate is fixed over the term of the loan.

Presumably, the increasing payments will be matched by increasing income due to inflation and real wage growth. This alleviates the dynamic mismatch associated with the FPM and resolves a good portion of the affordability problem.

The GPM was first authorized for Federal Housing Administration mortgages in 1977 under the FHA-245 program. The FHA-authorized GPM sets limits on the amount of graduation and limits the period of graduated payments to ten years. The maximum graduation rate is 7.5 percent annually for five years or 3 percent annually for ten years. These provisions are highly restrictive and, as experience with the instrument is gained, should be liberalized.

A variation on this theme is the equity-adjusted mortgage (EAM). Using this instrument the individual would contract with the mortgage lender to borrow on the identical terms that now apply, but a provision in the agreement would allow the borrower to receive automatically an additional loan each year equivalent to one-half the rate of inflation in the previous year multiplied by the amount of the mortgage principal outstanding at that time. The additional loan would, of course, be made at current market rates. After the amount necessary to amortize the additional annual loan has been taken into account, this loan could then be applied directly to mortgage payments due in that year. Alternatively, this equity withdrawal could be used for any other purpose.

Shared-Appreciation Mortgage.   Despite highly volatile interest and inflation rates, housing has been a remarkably good investment in the past ten years. This has promoted the use of SAMs by noninstitutional lenders. The FHLBB made a proposal to allow SLAs to issue SAMs in the fall of 1980. Comments were taken from the public, but as of early 1984 this type of instrument still cannot be made by regulated financial institutions.

The SAM offers the borrower a low rate of interest over a certain period in return for a specified share of property appreciation. The borrower and lender negotiate this tradeoff together with the term of the loan. The lender's share of appreciation is payable at the expiration of the loan or upon the sale or transfer of the property. If the property is not sold prior to loan maturity the amount of appreciation would be determined by an appraisal process. Since the actual appreciation rate is not known at the time the loan is made, the actual rate of return for the lender and the actual interest expense for the borrower are also not known in advance.

As in the case of the GPM, the SAM lowers the monthly payment to the household, allowing more households to qualify for home mortgages. The homeowner using a SAM is effectively borrowing against expected home appreciation as a means of entering the housing market. The SAM would be most appealing to first-time homebuyers who are willing to relinquish some of their potential appreciation to get into their first home.

The Dual-Interest-Rate Mortgage.   The DIM is simply a generalized version of the VRM and GPM. It sets two interest rates: one for the accrual rate by lenders on the mortgage debt and one that determines the borrower's payment rate.[2] The difference in the two implied payment streams would be added to or subtracted from the loan principal. To handle the lender's problem with the volatility and trend of interest rates, the accrual rate would be variable, with changes tied to a short- or medium-term Treasury obligation.

To handle the borrower's problem the payment rate could be set on a graduated basis. In essence, this DIM is really a variation of the graduated-payment adjustable-rate mortgage authorized in July 1981 by the FHLBB.

The DIM with a graduated payment rate appears to be the mortgage instrument with the best chance to solve both the lender's future profitability problems and the borrower's current affordability crisis. This instrument has been introduced by a number of lenders around the country and has such colorful names as certainly affordable mortgage plan (CAMEL).

Simulations of New Mortgage Instruments[3]

To examine the behavior of the new mortgage instruments, simulation experiments were performed with five commonly used or proposed loan types under three economic scenarios for the decade of the 1980s. The three economic scenarios assume different trends over the decade for the key variables in these simulations. The base scenario assumes a cyclical but essentially high level of inflation over the next decade (averaging 10% over the period) and a cyclical and slightly declining trend in interest rates from their 1982 levels. An accelerating inflation scenario assumes that short-term interest rates and inflation rates rise by 1 percent per year during the decade, to 19 percent by 1990. A decelerating inflation scenario, whereby interest and inflation rates drop by 5 percent over the decade, is also simulated. The key data to examine in calculating the effectiveness and riskiness of the mortgage are the payment-income ratio and the loan-to-current value ratio. This information is provided in Tables 7–8, 7–9, and 7–10.

Each simulation began with actual peak 1981 values for mortgage rates (17%), median house value ($68,420), median household income ($19,517), and six-month Treasury bill rates (14%). Each loan was assumed to be issued at an initial loan-to-value ratio of 80 percent for a term of thirty years.

The mortgage instruments examined include:

1. the traditional FPM;
2. a VRM in which the interest rate is indexed to the six-month Treasury bill rate and allowed to move without a cap;
3. a GPM in which payments increase 10 percent annually for the first ten years of the contract;
4. a SAM in which the lender receives 50 percent of the appreciated value of the property in exchange for reducing the mortgage rate by 40 percent; and
5. a dual-rate graduated-payment loan (DIM-GPM) in which payments increase 10 percent annually for the first ten years of the contract and the accrual rate is 2 percent over the six-month Treasury bill rate.[4]

Some interesting results emerge from these simulations. In the base scenario the affordability of housing is greatly improved under the GPM, SAM, and DIM-GPM instruments. Initial payment-income ratios are some 20 percent less than those of the FPM and VRM. By the end of the decade the payment-income ratio of the FPM falls to 20 percent, and the GPM remains at 29 percent. The SAM ratio is reduced to 12.8 percent, but a $65,000 cash payment would be due the lender if the property were sold in 1990. The DIM-GPM ratio falls to 23 percent, reflecting the reduction in interest rates inherent in this instrument. The VRM shows declining payments as a result of the stable and declining interest rate environment that is forecast. Negative amortization never exceeds 7 percent for any instrument —well within an acceptable risk level for an 80 percent loan.

Some problems began to surface with the DIM-GPM instruments in the accelerating inflation environment. The combination of relentlessly rising interest rates and the need to repay initial negative amortization, which lasts for five years in this case, produces a modest rise in the payment-income ratio over the decade. Although this situation would cause some problems if interest rates were to rise more rapidly in comparison with incomes, the problem could be reduced by decreasing allowed graduation from 10 to 5 percent annually. In this same environment the VRM shows a declining payment-income ratio as income growth more than offsets payment increases. Of course, the initial 48 percent income barrier for the VRM makes some type of GPM attractive.

In the decelerating inflation environment some unexpected results surface. With a steady drop of inflation to the 5 percent level, property values grow less than negative amortization in early years for the GPM and DIM-GPM instruments. As a result negative amortization gets as high as 12.5 percent —still acceptable on an 80 percent loan. This does imply, however, that a low down payment GPM loan with 10 percent graduation per year in a deflationary environment could increase default risk. Thus, the down payment constraint may outweigh the payment advantages of a GPM or DIM-GPM for some families. Again, the solution would be a somewhat slower graduation rate than the 10 percent used in these simulations.

Macro Impact of New Mortgage Instruments

It is apparent that the new mortgage instruments, especially the GPM, DIM-GPM, and SAM, can have a strong positive effect on the ability of first-time buyers to obtain mortgages. The VRM is neutral to slightly positive in this regard, depending on where the initial payment rate is set. So far VRM rates are being set between 1 and 1.5 percent below the FPM rate, making it easier to qualify for mortgage loans.

Table 7-8. Comparative Simulation of Various Alternative Mortgage Instruments (Base Forecast Scenario).

Year	Outstanding Principal	House Value[a]	Payment Rate[b]	Accrual Rate[c]	Income[d]	Payment as % of Income	Ratio of Loan to Value	Payments	Appreciation Due Lender
Fixed Rate Mortgage									
1981	54,651	68,420	17.00	17.00	19,517	48.11	79.88	9,390	0
1982	54,553	74,337	17.00	17.00	21,493	43.69	73.39	9,390	0
1983	54,437	82,932	17.00	17.00	23,622	39.75	65.64	9,390	0
1984	54,301	94,050	17.00	17.00	25,681	36.56	57.74	9,390	0
1985	54,143	106,858	17.00	17.00	28,053	33.47	50.67	9,390	0
1986	53,958	119,841	17.00	17.00	30,970	30.32	45.02	9,390	0
1987	53,741	135,054	17.00	17.00	34,184	27.47	39.79	9,390	0
1988	53,487	153,597	17.00	17.00	38,051	24.68	34.82	9,390	0
1989	53,190	175,883	17.00	17.00	42,421	22.13	30.24	9,390	0
1990	52,843	198,480	17.00	17.00	45,999	20.41	26.62	9,390	0
Variable Rate Mortgage									
1981	54,651	68,420	17.00	17.00	19,517	48.11	79.88	9,390	0
1982	54,484	74,337	14.27	14.25	21,493	37.01	73.29	7,995	0
1983	54,285	82,932	14.02	14.00	23,622	33.14	65.46	7,827	0
1984	54,124	94,050	15.97	16.00	25,681	34.45	57.55	8,846	0
1985	53,952	106,858	16.46	16.50	28,053	32.45	50.49	9,102	0
1986	53,718	119,841	15.50	15.50	30,970	27.76	44.82	8,597	0
1987	53,353	135,054	13.61	13.50	34,184	22.28	39.51	7,617	0
1988	52,994	153,597	14.54	14.50	38,051	21.28	34.50	8,096	0
1989	52,657	175,883	15.91	16.00	42,421	20.78	29.94	8,816	0
1990	52,185	198,480	14.56	14.50	45,999	17.62	26.29	8,107	0

Variable Rate with Cap

Year									
1981	54,651	68,420	17.00	17.00	19,517	48.11	79.88	9,390	0
1982	53,972	74,337	15.25	14.25	21,493	39.40	72.60	8,467	0
1983	53,774	82,932	13.88	14.00	23,622	32.82	64.84	7,754	0
1984	53,874	94,050	15.32	16.00	25,681	33.11	57.28	8,504	0
1985	53,703	106,858	16.38	16.50	28,053	32.30	50.26	9,060	0
1986	53,470	119,841	15.42	15.50	30,970	27.63	44.62	8,557	0
1987	52,967	135,054	13.81	13.50	34,184	22.59	39.22	7,721	0
1988	52,611	153,597	14.43	14.50	38,051	21.12	34.25	8,037	0
1989	52,276	175,883	15.79	16.00	42,421	20.63	29.72	8,752	0
1990	51,808	198,480	14.45	14.50	45,999	17.50	26.10	8,049	0

Graduated Payment Mortgage

Year									
1981	58,348	68,420	9.77	17.00	19,517	29.17	85.28	5,693	0
1982	62,004	74,337	10.93	17.00	21,493	29.14	83.41	6,263	0
1983	65,656	82,932	12.19	17.00	23,622	29.16	79.17	6,889	0
1984	69,239	94,050	13.54	17.00	25,681	29.51	73.62	7,578	0
1985	72,674	106,858	15.00	17.00	28,053	29.71	68.01	8,336	0
1986	75,860	119,841	16.59	17.00	30,970	29.61	63.30	9,169	0
1987	78,670	135,054	18.31	17.00	34,184	29.51	58.25	10,086	0
1988	80,948	153,597	20.19	17.00	38,051	29.16	52.70	11,095	0
1989	82,505	175,883	22.24	17.00	42,421	28.77	46.91	12,204	0
1990	83,107	198,480	24.49	17.00	45,999	29.18	41.87	13,425	0

Table 7-8. (Continued.)

Year	Outstanding Principal	House Value[a]	Payment Rate[b]	Accrual Rate[c]	Income[d]	Payment as % of Income	Ratio of Loan to Value	Payments	Appreciation Due Lender
Shared Appreciation Mortgage[e]									
1981	54,416	68,420	10.20	10.20	19,517	30.25	79.53	5,903	0
1982	54,063	74,337	10.20	10.20	21,493	27.47	76.71	5,903	2,959
1983	53,674	82,932	10.20	10.20	23,622	24.99	73.47	5,903	7,256
1984	53,245	94,050	10.20	10.20	25,681	22.99	70.24	5,903	12,815
1985	52,772	106,858	10.20	10.20	28,053	21.04	67.37	5,903	19,219
1986	52,252	119,841	10.20	10.20	30,970	19.06	65.05	5,903	25,711
1987	51,678	135,054	10.20	10.20	34,184	17.27	62.93	5,903	33,317
1988	51,046	153,597	10.20	10.20	38,051	15.51	60.96	5,903	42,589
1989	50,349	175,883	10.20	10.20	42,421	13.92	59.18	5,903	53,732
1990	49,581	198,480	10.20	10.20	45,999	12.83	57.74	5,903	65,030
Dual Rate Mortgage—GPM									
1981	56,979	68,420	9.77	14.50	19,517	29.17	83.28	5,693	0
1982	58,682	74,337	8.28	11.75	21,493	23.23	78.94	4,992	0
1983	60,272	82,932	8.64	11.50	23,622	21.84	72.68	5,159	0
1984	62,741	94,050	9.72	13.50	25,681	22.07	66.71	5,668	0
1985	65,150	106,858	11.16	14.00	28,053	22.72	60.97	6,374	0
1986	66,742	119,841	12.17	13.00	30,970	22.21	55.69	6,878	0
1987	66,922	135,054	12.72	11.00	34,184	20.95	49.55	7,161	0
1988	67,361	153,597	13.56	12.00	38,051	19.95	43.86	7,591	0
1989	67,955	175,883	15.31	13.50	42,421	20.04	38.64	8,500	0
1990	66,913	198,480	16.63	12.00	45,999	19.99	33.71	9,197	0

Dual Rate Mortgage — Standard Payment

Year									
1981	57,439	68,420	8.80	14.50	19,517	26.82	83.95	5,234	0
1982	58,878	74,337	8.96	11.75	21,493	24.70	79.20	5,310	0
1983	60,482	82,932	8.66	11.50	23,622	21.87	72.93	5,167	0
1984	63,116	94,050	9.43	13.50	25,681	21.54	67.11	5,531	0
1985	65,813	106,858	10.68	14.00	28,053	21.88	61.59	6,139	0
1986	67,893	119,841	11.36	13.00	30,970	20.91	56.65	6,476	0
1987	68,805	135,054	11.52	11.00	34,184	19.18	50.95	6,556	0
1988	70,490	153,597	11.55	12.00	38,051	17.27	45.89	6,572	0
1989	72,931	175,883	12.55	13.50	42,421	16.68	41.47	7,075	0
1990	74,111	198,480	13.52	12.00	45,999	16.46	37.34	7,572	0

Note: This is a simulation of six alternative mortgage instruments. Each mortgage has an original loan-to-value ratio of 80 percent calculated on the median existing home price for the first year of the simulation. The original maturity length of all mortgages is thirty years.

a House value is the median price of existing homes. Source: National Association of Realtors.

b The payment rate is the rate used to calculate monthly payments.

c The accrual rate is the rate used to calculate the outstanding balance of the loan.

d Income is the median household income from the Bureau of Census.

e For the shared-appreciation mortgage the balance used in calculating the loan-to-value ratio includes the lender's share of home price appreciation.

Table 7-9. Comparative Simulation of Various Alternative Mortgage Instruments (Accelerating Inflation Scenario).

Year	Out-standing Principal	House Value[a]	Payment Rate[b]	Accrual Rate[c]	Income[d]	Payment as % of Income	Ratio of Loan to Value	Payments	Appreciation Due Lender
Fixed Rate Mortgage									
1981	54,651	68,420	17.00	17.00	19,971	47.02	79.88	9,390	0
1982	54,553	75,946	17.00	17.00	22,167	42.36	71.83	9,390	0
1983	54,437	85,060	17.00	17.00	24,827	37.82	64.00	9,390	0
1984	54,301	96,118	17.00	17.00	28,055	33.47	56.49	9,390	0
1985	54,143	109,574	17.00	17.00	31,983	29.36	49.41	9,390	0
1986	53,958	126,010	17.00	17.00	36,780	25.53	42.82	9,390	0
1987	53,741	146,172	17.00	17.00	42,665	22.01	36.77	9,390	0
1988	53,487	171,021	17.00	17.00	49,918	18.81	31.28	9,390	0
1989	53,190	201,805	17.00	17.00	58,903	15.94	26.36	9,390	0
1990	52,843	240,147	17.00	17.00	70,094	13.40	22.00	9,390	0
Variable Rate Mortgage									
1981	54,651	68,420	17.00	17.00	19,971	47.02	79.88	9,390	0
1982	54,570	75,946	18.00	18.00	22,167	44.75	71.85	9,919	0
1983	54,490	85,060	18.99	19.00	24,827	42.08	64.06	10,448	0
1984	54,410	96,118	19.97	20.00	28,055	39.13	56.61	10,978	0
1985	54,329	109,574	20.95	21.00	31,983	35.98	49.58	11,507	0
1986	54,245	126,010	21.93	22.00	36,780	32.72	43.05	12,036	0
1987	54,158	146,172	22.91	23.00	42,665	29.45	37.05	12,564	0
1988	54,065	171,021	23.88	24.00	49,918	26.22	31.61	13,091	0
1989	53,965	201,805	24.85	25.00	58,903	23.12	26.74	13,617	0
1990	53,854	240,147	25.81	26.00	70,094	20.17	22.43	14,141	0

Variable Rate with Cap

1981	54,651	68,420	17.00	17.00	19,971	47.02	79.88	9,390	0
1982	54,570	75,946	18.00	18.00	22,167	44.75	71.85	9,919	0
1983	54,490	85,060	18.99	19.00	24,827	42.08	64.06	10,448	0
1984	54,410	96,118	19.97	20.00	28,055	39.13	56.61	10,978	0
1985	54,329	109,574	20.95	21.00	31,983	35.98	49.58	11,507	0
1986	54,245	126,010	21.93	22.00	36,780	32.72	43.05	12,036	0
1987	54,158	146,172	22.91	23.00	42,665	29.45	37.05	12,564	0
1988	54,065	171,021	23.88	24.00	49,918	26.22	31.61	13,091	0
1989	53,965	201,805	24.85	25.00	58,903	23.12	26.74	13,617	0
1990	53,854	240,147	25.81	26.00	70,094	20.17	22.43	14,141	0

Graduated Payment Mortgage

1981	58,348	68,420	9.77	17.00	19,971	28.51	85.28	5,693	0
1982	62,004	75,946	10.93	17.00	22,167	28.25	81.64	6,263	0
1983	65,656	85,060	12.19	17.00	24,827	27.75	77.19	6,889	0
1984	69,239	96,118	13.54	17.00	28,055	27.01	72.04	7,578	0
1985	72,674	109,574	15.00	17.00	31,983	26.06	66.32	8,336	0
1986	75,860	126,010	16.59	17.00	36,780	24.93	60.20	9,169	0
1987	78,670	146,172	18.31	17.00	42,665	23.64	53.82	10,086	0
1988	80,948	171,021	20.19	17.00	49,918	22.23	47.33	11,095	0
1989	82,505	201,805	22.24	17.00	58,903	20.72	40.88	12,204	0
1990	83,107	240,147	24.49	17.00	70,094	19.15	34.61	13,425	0

Table 7-9. (Continued.)

Year	Outstanding Principal	House Value[a]	Payment Rate[b]	Accrual Rate[c]	Income[d]	Payment as % of Income	Ratio of Loan to Value	Payments	Appreciation Due Lender
Shared Appreciation Mortgage[e]									
1981	54,416	68,420	10.20	10.20	19,971	29.56	79.53	5,903	0
1982	54,063	75,946	10.20	10.20	22,167	26.63	76.14	5,903	3,763
1983	53,674	85,060	10.20	10.20	24,827	23.78	72.88	5,903	8,320
1984	53,245	96,118	10.20	10.20	28,055	21.04	69.80	5,903	13,849
1985	52,772	109,574	10.20	10.20	31,983	18.46	66.94	5,903	20,577
1986	52,252	126,010	10.20	10.20	36,780	16.05	64.32	5,903	28,795
1987	51,678	146,172	10.20	10.20	42,665	13.84	61.95	5,903	38,876
1988	51,046	171,021	10.20	10.20	49,918	11.83	59.84	5,903	51,301
1989	50,349	201,805	10.20	10.20	58,903	10.02	58.00	5,903	66,693
1990	49,581	240,147	10.20	10.20	70,094	8.42	56.40	5,903	85,864
Dual Rate Mortgage—GPM									
1981	56,979	68,420	9.77	14.50	19,971	28.51	83.28	5,693	0
1982	59,695	75,946	10.64	15.50	22,167	27.59	78.60	6,116	0
1983	62,912	85,060	11.68	16.50	24,827	26.71	73.96	6,632	0
1984	66,661	96,118	12.92	17.50	28,055	25.88	69.35	7,261	0
1985	70,968	109,574	14.40	18.50	31,983	25.09	64.77	8,025	0
1986	75,853	126,010	16.18	19.50	36,780	24.34	60.20	8,954	0
1987	81,317	146,172	18.30	20.50	42,665	23.64	55.63	10,085	0
1988	87,332	171,021	20.88	21.50	49,918	22.97	51.07	11,468	0
1989	93,815	201,805	24.02	22.50	58,903	22.35	46.49	13,167	0
1990	100,596	240,147	27.87	23.50	70,094	21.78	41.89	15,265	0

Dual Rate Mortgage – Standard Payment

Year									
1981	57,439	68,420	8.80	14.50	19,971	26.21	83.95	5,234	0
1982	60,832	75,946	9.38	15.50	22,167	24.86	80.10	5,510	0
1983	65,113	85,060	9.90	16.50	24,827	23.19	76.55	5,757	0
1984	70,013	96,118	11.40	17.50	28,055	23.15	72.84	6,494	0
1985	75,621	109,574	13.08	18.50	31,983	22.97	69.01	7,345	0
1986	82,196	126,010	14.68	19.50	36,780	22.22	65.23	8,171	0
1987	89,551	146,172	17.20	20.50	42,665	22.26	61.26	9,495	0
1988	97,971	171,021	19.70	21.50	49,918	21.70	57.29	10,883	0
1989	107,617	201,805	22.60	22.50	58,903	21.05	53.33	12,397	0
1990	118,676	240,147	25.97	23.50	70,094	20.30	49.42	14,231	0

Note: This is a simulation of six alternative mortgage instruments. Each mortgage has an original loan-to-value ratio of 80 percent calculated on the median existing home price for the first year of the simulation. The original maturity length of all mortgages is thirty years.

a House value is the median price of existing homes. Source: National Association of Realtors.

b The payment rate is the rate used to calculate monthly payments.

c The accrual rate is the rate used to calculate the outstanding balance of the loan.

d Income is the median household income from the Bureau of Census.

e For the shared-appreciation mortgage the balance used in calculating the loan-to-value ratio includes the lender's share of home price appreciation.

Table 7-10. Comparative Simulation of Various Alternative Mortgage Instruments (Decelerating Inflation Scenario).

Year	Outstanding Principal	House Value[a]	Payment Rate[b]	Accrual Rate[c]	Income[d]	Payment as % of Income	Ratio of Loan to Value	Payments	Appreciation Due Lender
Fixed Rate Mortgage									
1981	52,167	65,310	17.00	17.00	19,971	44.88	79.88	8,963	0
1982	52,073	68,412	17.00	17.00	21,868	40.99	76.12	8,963	0
1983	51,962	71,491	17.00	17.00	23,836	37.60	72.68	8,963	0
1984	51,833	74,529	17.00	17.00	25,862	34.66	69.55	8,963	0
1985	51,682	77,510	17.00	17.00	27,931	32.09	66.68	8,963	0
1986	51,505	80,417	17.00	17.00	30,026	29.85	64.05	8,963	0
1987	51,298	83,232	17.00	17.00	32,127	27.90	61.63	8,963	0
1988	51,056	85,937	17.00	17.00	34,216	26.19	59.41	8,963	0
1989	50,772	88,515	17.00	17.00	36,269	24.71	57.36	8,963	0
1990	50,441	90,949	17.00	17.00	38,263	23.42	55.46	8,963	0
Variable Rate Mortgage									
1981	52,167	65,310	17.00	17.00	19,971	44.88	79.88	8,963	0
1982	52,063	68,412	16.50	16.50	21,868	39.84	76.10	8,712	0
1983	51,931	71,491	16.01	16.00	23,836	35.50	72.64	8,463	0
1984	51,763	74,529	15.52	15.50	25,862	31.77	69.45	8,217	0
1985	51,552	77,510	15.03	15.00	27,931	28.55	66.51	7,975	0
1986	51,290	80,417	14.56	14.50	30,026	25.77	63.78	7,737	0
1987	50,967	83,232	14.08	14.00	32,127	23.36	61.23	7,504	0
1988	50,571	85,937	13.62	13.50	34,216	21.26	58.85	7,276	0
1989	50,092	88,515	13.17	13.00	36,269	19.45	56.59	7,054	0
1990	49,516	90,949	12.73	12.50	38,263	17.87	54.44	6,838	0

Variable Rate with Cap

1981	52,167	65,310	17.00	17.00	19,971	44.88	79.88	8,963	0
1982	52,063	68,412	16.50	16.50	21,868	39.84	76.10	8,712	0
1983	51,931	71,491	16.01	16.00	23,836	35.50	72.64	8,463	0
1984	51,763	74,529	15.52	15.50	25,862	31.77	69.45	8,217	0
1985	51,552	77,510	15.03	15.00	27,931	28.55	66.51	7,975	0
1986	51,290	80,417	14.56	14.50	30,026	25.77	63.78	7,737	0
1987	50,967	83,232	14.08	14.00	32,127	23.36	61.23	7,504	0
1988	50,571	85,937	13.62	13.50	34,216	21.26	58.85	7,276	0
1989	50,092	88,515	13.17	13.00	36,269	19.45	56.59	7,054	0
1990	49,516	90,949	12.73	12.50	38,263	17.87	54.44	6,838	0

Graduated Payment Mortgage

1981	55,696	65,310	9.77	17.00	19,971	27.21	85.28	5,435	0
1982	59,186	68,412	10.93	17.00	21,868	27.34	86.51	5,978	0
1983	62,671	71,491	12.19	17.00	23,836	27.59	87.66	6,576	0
1984	66,092	74,529	13.54	17.00	25,862	27.97	88.68	7,233	0
1985	69,371	77,510	15.00	17.00	27,931	28.49	89.50	7,957	0
1986	72,411	80,417	16.59	17.00	30,026	29.15	90.04	8,753	0
1987	75,094	83,232	18.31	17.00	32,127	29.97	90.22	9,628	0
1988	77,269	85,937	20.19	17.00	34,216	30.95	89.91	10,591	0
1989	78,755	88,515	22.24	17.00	36,269	32.12	89.97	11,650	0
1990	79,329	90,949	24.49	17.00	38,263	33.49	87.22	12,815	0

Table 7-10. (Continued.)

Year	Out-standing Principal	House Value[a]	Payment Rate[b]	Accrual Rate[c]	Income[d]	Payment as % of Income	Ratio of Loan to Value	Payments	Appreciation Due Lender
Shared Appreciation Mortgage[e]									
1981	51,942	65,310	10.20	10.20	19,971	28.22	79.53	5,635	0
1982	51,605	68,412	10.20	10.20	21,868	25.77	77.70	5,635	1,551
1983	51,234	71,491	10.20	10.20	23,836	23.64	75.99	5,635	3,091
1984	50,825	74,529	10.20	10.20	25,862	21.79	74.38	5,635	4,610
1985	50,374	77,510	10.20	10.20	27,931	20.18	72.86	5,635	6,100
1986	49,877	80,417	10.20	10.20	30,026	18.77	71.42	5,635	7,554
1987	49,329	83,232	10.20	10.20	32,127	17.54	70.03	5,635	8,961
1988	48,725	85,937	10.20	10.20	34,216	16.47	68.70	5,635	10,314
1989	48,060	88,515	10.20	10.20	36,269	15.54	67.40	5,635	11,603
1990	47,327	90,949	10.20	10.20	38,263	14.73	66.13	5,635	12,820
Dual Rate Mortgage—GPM									
1981	53,606	65,310	9.77	13.00	19,971	27.21	82.08	5,435	0
1982	54,553	68,412	10.46	12.50	21,868	26.31	79.74	5,754	0
1983	55,038	71,491	11.11	12.00	23,836	25.43	76.99	6,061	0
1984	55,015	74,529	11.72	11.50	25,862	24.56	73.82	6,352	0
1985	54,443	77,510	12.29	11.00	27,931	23.71	70.24	6,623	0
1986	53,291	80,417	12.79	10.50	30,026	22.88	66.27	6,869	0
1987	51,534	83,232	13.24	10.00	32,127	22.05	61.92	7,085	0
1988	49,162	85,937	13.61	9.50	34,216	21.24	57.21	7,268	0
1989	46,175	88,515	13.90	9.00	36,269	20.44	52.17	7,412	0
1990	42,586	90,949	14.11	8.50	38,263	19.64	46.82	7,513	0

Dual Rate Mortgage—Standard Payment

1981	54,045	65,310	8.80	13.00	19,971	25.01	82.75	4,996	0
1982	55,730	68,412	8.96	12.50	21,868	23.18	81.46	5,070	0
1983	57,489	71,491	8.65	12.00	23,836	20.68	80.41	4,929	0
1984	59,076	74,529	8.86	11.50	25,862	19.43	79.27	5,025	0
1985	60,463	77,510	9.05	11.00	27,931	18.30	78.01	5,111	0
1986	61,623	80,417	9.23	10.50	30,026	17.28	76.63	5,188	0
1987	62,530	83,232	9.37	10.00	32,127	16.36	75.13	5,256	0
1988	63,158	85,937	9.50	9.50	34,216	15.53	73.49	5,313	0
1989	63,482	88,515	9.60	9.00	36,269	14.78	71.72	5,360	0
1990	63,482	90,949	-9.68	8.50	38,263	14.10	69.80	5,396	0

Note: This is a simulation of six alternative mortgage instruments. Each mortgage has an original loan-to-value ratio of 80 percent calculated on the median existing home price for the first year of the simulation. The original maturity length of all mortgages is thirty years.

a House value is the median price of existing homes. Source: National Association of Realtors.

b The payment rate is the rate used to calculate monthly payments.

c The accrual rate is the rate used to calculate the outstanding balance of the loan.

d Income is the median household income from the Bureau of Census.

e For the shared-appreciation mortgage the balance used in calculating the loan-to-value ratio includes the lender's share of home price appreciation.

The VRM instrument also appears to be having a positive supply effect on the mortgage market. Since this instrument allows mortgage rates to adjust more rapidly to changes in overall market interest rates, it lets the mortgage market clear through changes in prices rather than through credit rationing. Also, since the return on the outstanding portfolio of mortgage holdings of lenders adjusts to changing open market rates, the volatility of capital gains and losses on such a portfolio is substantially reduced. As a result the VRM could cause a substantial moderation of cyclical fluctuations in the mortgage and housing markets by increasing and stabilizing the supply of mortgage credit.

Widespread use of VRMs and DIM-GPMs could, however, induce several macroeconomic problems. First, there may be a critical demand-side influence of a more flexible mortgage interest rate. Since there is a fairly sensitive response of housing starts to changes in mortgage rates, the greater variance of mortgage rates in the variable-rate world could increase cyclical instability. Second, since mortgage interest rates on existing as well as new loans would be flexible, the demand for the entire housing stock would be subject to fluctuations. While it is too early to assess the extent of these potential macroeconomic problems, the ability of these new instruments to alleviate the affordability and profitability problems would appear to outweigh the potential risks.

Deregulation of the mortgage instrument promises a solution to serious problems facing the housing finance system. Without doubt, expansion in choice of mortgage instruments improves the welfare of both the consumer and the lender.

NOTES

1. In the initial years of a GPM it is conceivable that payments may not even cover interest charges on the principal. In such a case the deficiency is added to the principal amount of the loan and future payments are adjusted upward. This situation is known as "negative amortization," and it is equivalent to the automatic provision of additional loans.

2. In the conventional fixed-payment fixed-rate loan the accrual and amortization rates are equal.

3. The assistance of Karen Alpert in running these simulations is gratefully acknowledged.

4. The accrual rate is the rate used to calculate the outstanding balance of the loan. In contrast, the payment rate is the rate used to calculate monthly payments.

Chapter 8

New Directions for Housing and Mortgage Policy in the 1980s

The current predicament of the housing industry has been extensively detailed in preceding chapters. Demographic and sociological changes will put an unprecedented burden on the housing production system while it is still reeling from the effects of the severe economic turmoil that marked the end of the 1970s and beginning of the 1980s. The costs of regulation of the housing industry and the housing finance system over the past two decades are now appearing with a vengeance, threatening to undermine the future of this sector of the economy unless public policies are significantly revised. This situation has emerged at a time when the executive branch of the federal government has announced its intention — for ideological and fiscal reasons — to deemphasize the role of the national government in domestic affairs.

While the free market rhetoric is generally persuasive, it should not be used here as an excuse to disinherit the housing industry, which is in need of well-tailored policies to ease the transition from a regulated environment to a competitive regime for investment in housing. In addition, it would be inappropriate and unjust to abandon the long-standing national goal of ensuring adequate shelter for the citizenry. Accordingly, there is a significant and active role for the federal government in shaping and implementing housing policy for the 1980s.

COUNTERCYCLICAL POLICIES

The collapse of housing markets in the 1980–82 period was primarily a result of excessively tight monetary policy. Growth in nominal GNP was not matched by additional money, creating credit shortages and some of the

161

highest real interest rates in the history of our nation. The only two other periods of comparable real rates were during the great depressions of the 1870s and 1930s. As a result the housing market in the early 1980s was devastated. Housing demand and production are intrinsically linked to the availability of long-term credit, and the result of these macroeconomic conditions was a complete collapse of new and existing home sales markets.

The extreme volatility of interest and money supply growth rates since late 1979 was produced by unacceptable monetary policy. The Federal Reserve Board (FRB) must, therefore, pursue a more moderate real interest rate policy during the transition period. Attempts to adhere to "black box" monetary targets are indefensible, given the problems these policies create, not just for the housing sector but throughout the economy.

Federal agencies must continue countercyclical mortgage credit supply programs during this transition period. The Government National Mortgage Association (GNMA) was used very effectively, although slowly, for just this purpose during the housing recession of 1974–75. The Federal National Mortgage Association (FNMA) and Federal Home Loan Mortgage Association (FHLMC) were also effective in pumping money into the market during this period of credit tightness. In the 1980–82 period there was little attempt to use countercyclical programs to remedy the problems of the housing and mortgage markets, and the administration has actually disavowed any intention to offer such countercyclical aid.

The crisis of the early 1980s was so severe, however, that it required a new countercyclical strategy. In the past most of the difficulty was produced by the lack of money in the hands of credit suppliers. In the early 1980s high real and nominal mortgage interest rates were responsible. Countercyclical assistance to housing must therefore provide a temporary mortgage interest rate reduction if it is to be effective in moderating the down side of the housing cycle. A mortgage buydown program, whereby the government provides a small amount of upfront money to reduce the mortgage rate by two to four percentage points, could be quite effective in the new environment. This temporary subsidy for one to three years could be used to leverage the available private sector credit.

This shallow or temporary interest subsidy program, run through several of the secondary mortgage agencies, could provide part of the solution to the short-run cyclical homebuilding problem likely to be experienced in the 1980s. This new strategy is motivated by the fact that housing cycles of the mid- and late 1980s will be due to fluctuations in the price of credit rather than to variations in the availability of credit, as was characteristic of housing cycles in the 1970s. Although these initiatives would be only moderately effective because housing still competes with other capital demands, the government has an important role to play in providing countercyclical assistance.

THE PLIGHT OF THE THRIFTS

For most of this century thrift institutions have been the mainstay of the housing finance supply system, but in the 1980–82 period they were in extreme distress. Most of the responsibility for this situation could have been assigned to past regulations that inefficiently restricted their activities. While these constraints have been eased or eliminated in the past several years, the continued existence of the thrift industry as a major source of housing credit may require prompt federal action during this transition period.

During the period of peak interest rate the thrifts had an unrealized portfolio loss of more than $150 billion—the amount by which they would fall short if they were forced to monetize all their present assets to pay off all their present liabilities. This was caused because market yields on deposits rose dramatically while asset yields rose only modestly. If short-term interest rates were again to rise to the 12 to 14 percent vicinity, as they did for much of 1981 and 1982, as many as one-third of all thrift institutions would exhaust their regulatory net worth, which was decimated by the 1980–82 experience, within a year. Regulations require that thrift institutions demonstrate, at minimum, a 3 percent net worth. Obviously, this is an inoperative constraint, as some thrift institutions violated it but were permitted to continue their operations. All the net worth measure does is tell how much of a loss has been taken so far by the thrifts. The actual net worth of most SLAs in 1981–82 was in the range of −25 to −35 percent—because of their past unrealized portfolio losses.

The problem was really one of investor confidence, and the solution was directed at bolstering the confidence in these depository institutions. In 1982 the federal government authorized the "net worth certificates" for those institutions falling below the minimum regulatory net worth constraint. This formalized the role of the federal government in supporting the thrift industry, which increased the confidence of potential depositors.

As long as their mortgage loans are paid off promptly and Savings and Loan Associations (SLAs) have a cash flow sufficient to meet depositor demands, the actual negative net worth does not matter. SLAs merely have to retain the confidence of depositors. The sharp decline in interest rates since the summer of 1982 has made widespread use of these certificates unnecessary. However, during the next interest rate surge they could be used extensively.

Changes in tax laws could also provide resources to help subsidize the lending industry and the consumer. This would involve the imposition of capital gains taxes on housing, equivalent to the capital gains taxes applied to other forms of investment. This tax would primarily affect those housing consumers who gained from the sharp escalation of housing prices in the past decade. The proceeds could be earmarked for subsidizing interest rates for first-time homebuyers or supplementing the net worth of SLAs.

This proposal would entail an elimination of the large exclusion and roll-over provision on long-term gains for housing, bringing the maximum tax rate on housing appreciation to 20 percent. The roll-over provision of the tax law allows those who sell their homes to transfer the profits from that transaction into the purchase of another home without taxation. Allowing the large increment in housing values of the last decade to go untaxed has caused distortions in the housing sector. This preferential treatment of housing investment may actually have caused some of the price escalation recently observed.

Needless to say, this is a very controversial proposal. On the one hand, subsidies to first-time buyers or troubled thrifts to be supported by the proceeds of such a tax look attractive. On the other hand, the increased taxes on ownership transfers would reduce resale volume. Present homeowners would be less inclined to move into larger and more costly units.

One problem with this proposal is that it changes the rules of housing market investment retroactively. In the final analysis borrowers and lenders were betting against each other on the way the housing market would evolve over the term of a mortgage. Each of these parties entered into the transaction with some expectation about the perpetuity of relevant laws and regulations. Additionally, each had expectations about future market trends. In the present situation it appears that borrowers, by wit or fortune, placed good bets in the 1970s. Retroactive repeal of the 1970s housing market "rules" would, under this argument, unfairly penalize those who made good choices and reward those who chose poorly. The same argument, however, also holds for the enforcement of the "due-on-sale" clause.

The Gain–St. Germain bill, passed in the fall of 1982 to aid the ailing thrift industry, dictated the enforcement of the due-on-sale clause incorporated in most mortgages issued by thrift institutions in the past decade. Approximately seventeen states did not allow enforcement of the due-on-sale clause, which mandates full repayment of the existing mortgage loan when property transfers hands. If the due-on-sale provision could be enforced then presumably a new mortgage, at prevailing interest rates, would be issued to finance the purchase by the new owner. This would obviously be in the interest of mortgage providers when interest rates are rising. Conversely, enforcement of the due-on-sale provision would restrict the options of existing homeowners who could not capitalize their low-interest, fixed-rate mortgage.

In most instances borrowers did not explicitly pay for the privilege of transferring their mortgage to the subsequent owner of the property. If the clause were not enforced, the low-cost mortgage would probably be held by the original and subsequent owners of the property until full maturity, exacerbating the portfolio imbalance problem of the thrift institutions that issued many of these loans. Court rulings superseding due-on-sale clauses caused lenders to incur large, unforeseen losses by extending the life of low-rate mortgages. The national override, permitting enforcement of the due-on-sale provision, was good public policy in this situation. People should, of course, be afforded the opportunity to purchase an assumability clause in newly originated mortgages if they so desire. Such a provision might entail a 1 or 2 percent mortgage rate premium, but it could be a worthwhile investment.

There were many critics of this national override policy. The real estate community was divided: although it might help existing mortgage lenders, it might adversely affect the existing home resale market. In 1981–82, 60 to 70 percent of all resales used assumable mortgages as a means of lowering the cost to first-time homebuyers. However, the Gain–St. Germain legislation made it clear that national housing policy must directly confront the first-time buyer problem rather than force SLAs and banks to bear the burden of judicial decisions that ignored the economic realities of mortgage lending. Difficulty in completing home transactions in an era of high interest rates should be confronted by specific policies to lower rates or otherwise assist in lowering payments, but not a policy that decimates the financial system that has supported housing so well.

Another policy that should be continued is the federal override of usury law ceilings. Financial reform legislation passed in 1980 superseded state usury laws for a period of three years, after which time states could re-institute these ceilings. All the research in this area indicates that usury law ceilings inefficiently limit the amount of mortgage credit that is offered by providers and prevent loans from being made to riskier borrowers — low- and middle-income households.

Again, this is a situation in which something that seemed like an appropriate consumer protection measure has, in effect, created disarray in the long-term market for mortgage credit. National housing policy must work through markets, providing direct subsidies to those who need assistance rather than trying to provide indirect subsidies through regulations and regulatory constraints on interest rates. In order to have an efficient and competitive financial system it is necessary to have a market system with direct subsidies rather than subsidies provided by regulations.

The housing finance system could also be aided by the easing of restrictions on interstate and interindustry mergers, to the extent that they are consistent with administration and Federal Home Loan Bank (FHLB) policies. Institutions that are healthy and have a positive net worth should be encouraged to take over less healthy institutions. Given the highly fragmented nature of our financial system, such consolidations would not restrict competition in the deposit and mortgage markets, and consumers could well benefit from the economies of scale in larger banking units.

A coordinated plan for consolidation of SLAs should be developed by the Federal Deposit Insurance Corporation (FDIC), the Federal Savings and Loans Insurance Corporation, the FHLBB, and the FRB. This plan should also allow for timely and appropriate mergers with CBs. Insofar as it is possible, market factors should be allowed to shape this consolidation plan. A haphazard strategy based on rescuing institutions that happen to be failing makes little sense.

Thrift institutions must themselves be permitted to diversify, in the sense that deregulation of asset portfolios should be continued and extended. Thrift institutions were forced by past regulation to put too many of their eggs in a single basket—the residential mortgage market. Specialization of this sort increases risk and the susceptibility of institutions to unfavorable, localized market conditions. Portfolio diversification is the first principle of finance learned by those interested in moderating their sensitivity to market forces. Presumably, a fully diversified thrift institution would benefit from a reduced cost of funds as depositors would attach a more modest risk premium to their interest rate demands. Some portion of this benefit may pass through to the mortgage borrower as thrifts attempt to compete more effectively by lowering their own required rate of return.

ENHANCING THE AFFORDABILITY OF HOUSING

In the 1980s affordability will continue to be the basic problem facing entrants to the housing market; the problem is particularly severe for first-time homebuyers. The affordability problem for housing purchasers is a combination of high initial payment-to-income ratios, which tend to disqualify large numbers of potential buyers under traditional mortgage-lending criteria, and continued large down payment requirements.

The first of these aspects can be addressed by changing either the income available to households or the way monthly mortgage payments are calculated. Available income can be altered by direct transfers or by public policies that endeavor to reduce capital market inefficiencies that limit the ability of households to borrow against their future income. Payments can be directly altered by the use of new mortgage instruments.

Both of these approaches recognize that a large part of the housing affordability problem is artificially created by the inflation premium built into mortgage interest rates and the inflexibility of the level-payment mortgage. Shared-appreciation mortgages (SAMs) and equity-adjusted mortgages (EAMs) in effect allow households to implicitly (through reduced payments) or explicitly (through actual annual loans) borrow against the expected appreciation of their properties. Graduated-payment mortgages (GPMs) also provide for a better matching of payments to income over time by allowing lower payments in the initial years of a mortgage, which then increase annually at a specified rate for a specified number of years. Variable-rate mortgages (VRMs) operate by pegging mortgage rates and payments over the term of the loan to interest rate indices. Since this feature would partially insulate them from financial market fluctuations, lenders could offer these loans at somewhat lower initial rates to reflect the lowered risk. This also reduces initial payments and improves affordability. The dual-interest-rate mortgage with a graduated-payment mechanism (DIM-GPM) also provides implicit loans to purchasers (through the accumulation of negative amortization) and lower payments in early years. This type of mortgage loan is thought to hold the most promise for resolving affordability problems in the 1980s.

The federal government should make aggressive use of FHA programs to popularize these new instruments. At this time the Federal Housing Administration (FHA) has not taken a strong leadership position in this experimentation and education process. The FHA, working in conjunction with private mortgage insurance companies, should develop a small number of standardized instruments that can be marketed through the GNMA, FNMA, and FHLMC guarantee programs.

Hedging techniques should also be encouraged, allowing borrowers and lenders to insure themselves against future interest rate fluctuations. Individuals are fond of stability, and they should be provided the opportunity to purchase stable mortgage rates or payments at a reasonable price. Considerable consumer and lender education efforts may be required before new mortgages and interest rate hedging techniques gain acceptance, and it is an appropriate task for government during the transition to the new housing market of the 1980s.

Affordability for first-time purchasers could be improved by switching from the present tax deduction treatment of mortgage interest payments to a program of tax credits. One proposal would replace the interest deduction provision of federal income tax law with a graduated tax credit that would allow first-time purchasers to reduce their tax obligation in the first year of a mortgage by an amount equal to the total mortgage interest payments in that year. The proportion of mortgage interest that could be used to offset taxes would be reduced to zero over time and a ceiling on the amount of credit in any one year could also be specified.

This scheme would make federal tax treatment of mortgage interest far more equitable than the deduction system that allows those with the highest incomes and house values to receive the largest benefits. By converting to a tax credit, everyone would get the same percentage credit regardless of income. This tax credit would be targeted so that it would primarily benefit first-time buyers. As people become mature homeowners and accumulate wealth their tax credit will decline substantially. The tax credit gap would eliminate very high priced real estate from the deduction and further improve the equity of the tax treatment of housing.

The other major part of the affordability problem is that first-time home-buyers must somehow accumulate large down payments to purchase a house. This difficulty could be addressed directly by providing a larger volume of low-rate down payment loans through the FHA or Veterans' Administration (VA), again restricted to first-time buyers. The loans, which would involve government insurance and would be provided by the government, would then be sold to the private secondary market.

An alternative favored in many European countries is to initiate a savings for housing plan. A proposal the author made in 1977 would allow households to set up individual housing accounts (IHAs). The IHA would assist the moderate-income, first-time homebuyer in accumulating the substantial down payment required to purchase a new home.

To illustrate, households with adjusted gross incomes of less than $20,000 might be allowed to deduct up to $2,500 per year from their gross income and put this money in an IHA. They would be allowed to accumulate up to $10,000 in this account over time. After an initial one-year holding period the household would be allowed to withdraw this money and use it toward the purchase of a home. Provided that the IHA is applied to the purchase of a home, no tax would be paid on this sum or the interest income that had accrued in the account. These special IHAs would be restricted to first-time homebuyers, as this group would not have had the advantage of equity accumulation in an existing home.

The IHA idea is quite similar to the individual retirement accounts (IRAs). The same set of institutions would presumably respond to this incentive scheme; however, the individuals participating would be very different. Since the program would be restricted to first-time homebuyers with incomes less than $20,000, it would benefit young and low- to moderate-income households.

Another possible way of doing this would be through an expanded IRA approach. Existing IRAs could be used for either first-time home purchase or retirement. As in the IHA proposal, no tax would be assessed on these funds if they were applied to the purchase of a house. The amount of money accumulated in the account could be used as a down payment. It would be deducted from the basic cost of the property and the tax would be recaptured at some point in the future when the house is finally sold. Given that we already have the IRA accounts, it would be more efficient to let people use an expanded IRA concept than to set up separate individual housing accounts.

The major objection to this idea is that it may result in a loss of tax revenues. The tax loss associated with these earmarked savings accounts would be quite small, since it would only lead to a deferral of tax receipts, just as with the IRA, and it would tend to involve those in lower and middle-class income groups. Despite this revenue loss ($1 to $2 billion annually), a savings for housing plan would be a valuable tool, allowing the government to stimulate housing without disrupting the entire set of financial markets and providing a direct subsidy to the most disadvantaged households in the housing market.

MODERATION OF LAND-USE AND
RENT CONTROLS

In addition to demand-side initiatives to increase the affordability of housing, there is also a need for policies aimed directly at the problem of high housing prices. Over the past decade house prices have risen relative to the price of other goods primarily as a result of a supply-demand imbalance in the housing markets. A set of programs is needed to remove the regulations and constraints that inhibit the supply of new construction creating this imbalance.

The major set of constraints have been at the local level—land-use and growth controls. These growth management systems inhibit new growth either by imposing fees directly on homebuilders or by not allowing building to occur. They serve to drive up the price of land and therefore the price of housing. Growth and land-use controls can make as much as a 20 percent difference in the price of housing in metropolitan areas.

Since these controls are traditionally in the province of local and state governments, drafting a national policy in this regard is difficult. State governments should seriously consider the introduction of state zoning override provisions, perhaps through the creation of an appeals board for developers, builders, and others concerned with housing production.

This process could encourage planned growth and reasonable development goals rather than a no-growth philosophy or haphazard and environmentally unsound growth. Thus, a strong state appeals board or regional appeals board system could be the solution to the land-use problem, putting the onus of allowing adequate housing on the community as well as the developer and builder. Communities must be made to realize that the post–World War II baby boom generation must be housed. While it may mean higher densities and more congestion, adequate and sufficient housing is an essential element of our national economic policy.

Rent control is another locally controlled policy that inhibits housing production. Even though rents have not been rising faster than the rate of inflation, they are rising faster than the incomes of some people, especially the elderly. This problem has caused a clamor for rent control in some areas. Rent control clearly has some short-term positive benefits for tenants, but in the long run society is substantially worse off because of lower levels of housing production and reduced maintenance of the existing housing stock.

The rent control problem probably is best handled by a nationwide override of rent control similar to the nationwide override of usury law ceilings. If a nationwide override were not enacted, each state might be encouraged to provide a statewide override of rent control. An override that would be binding both at the state and national level is essential to convince lenders and potential investors to put their money into rental housing. If the rate of return on rental housing is depressed below the return on other assets, new production of rental housing will be reduced.

Conservation of the existing rental housing stock is an essential objective of national housing policy. Rehabilitation tax incentives (e.g., tax credits) similar to those provided for the commercial sector must be extended to rental housing to prevent wholesale conversion of residential rental stock to commercial uses and to encourage conversion of dilapidated commercial stock to residential use.

The President's Commission on Housing has made such a recommendation. These tax credits, at a level of 15 to 20 percent of rehabilitation expenditures, would do much to improve that part of the rental housing stock that is deteriorating rapidly. It would also create incentives for people to convert commercial structures to residential structures and reduce perverse incentives to convert residential units to commercial structures because of the present asymmetry in tax treatment.

New financing techniques can also be used to encourage a larger supply of rental housing. Developers and investors in the rental sector should also be able to use combination graduated-payment variable-rate mortgages. The rental sector has the same inflation premium built into the mortgage interest rate that afflicts purchasers, making it difficult for projects to look economically feasible based on first-year payment-to-rent ratios. The GPM would make rental projects look much more attractive. Again, as in the case of homeownership affordability, there is an early cash flow problem that a new mortgage instrument can alleviate. The government should take the lead in providing graduated-payment variable-rate mortgages for the rental sector and educating the rental sector lenders on the advantages of such a mortgage.

AVAILABILITY OF MORTGAGE CREDIT

Housing policy should be designed to stimulate an adequate supply of mortgage credit, especially with the phasing out of the specialized set of financial institutions for housing. There appears to be a consensus that a mortgage tax credit for any individual or institution that invests in mortgages is the best way to proceed.

A mortgage tax credit of 10 to 15 percent of the amount of interest received would encourage lenders to invest in mortgages. In the case of lenders who do not have tax liabilities — pension or not-for-profit organizations — a refundable tax credit might be necessary. The net effect would be to lower mortgage interest rates. People want a rate of return on mortgages equivalent to what is paid by other assets. Allowing a tax credit raises the effective rate of return on the mortgage. If this were done, tax-exempt mortgage revenue bonds and some of the specialized provisions for SLAs could be eliminated. It would only be a matter of fine tuning the system and determining the right level of tax credit needed to obtain an adequate supply of mortgage credit. Although such adjustments would have to be done within a dynamic supply and demand framework, a tax credit that was adjusted yearly would be a plausible policy.

CONCLUSION

Housing and mortgage policies of the 1980s must address the new and vital needs and problems of the housing market. These problems include the affordability crisis of the first-time homebuyer and the recurrent profitability crisis of the thrift institutions. The cyclical volatility of housing has to be moderated, not only through better macroeconomic policy but through a specific set of countercyclical housing programs. The spiraling cost of housing must be contained by encouraging new production and overriding excessively stringent local land-use and rent control. The government must provide leadership in devising new mortgage instruments and educating borrowers and lenders. Tax incentives for housing and mortgages must be more precisely targeted to produce the desired results.

The process of moving from a set of policies based on stability, low inflation, and low real interest rates — policies that worked well for fifty years — to this tax incentive, private-sector-oriented regime will be painful. There is a large potential that transition to a deregulated housing industry and housing finance system will not proceed smoothly. However, there is no doubt that we need to revamp the present system if we are to meet the needs of the tremendous number of people coming into the housing market in the 1980s.

Adequate and affordable housing for the maturing post–World War II baby boom generation is essential if we are to meet our obligations to the current generation of young Americans. Homeownership is a critical building block for our democratic system. Ignoring the *shelter* (rather than investment) demand for owner-occupied housing in the 1980s could create a major political and economic crisis. The new policy initiatives put forth in this book could go a long way toward averting this crisis.

*

Abbreviations and Acronyms

ABAG	Association of Bay Area Governments
AHS	*Annual Housing Survey*
AML	adjustable mortgage loan
ARM	adjustable rate mortgage
ASC	all savers certificate
CAMEL	certainly affordable mortgage loan
CB	commercial bank
CPI	consumer price index
CREUE	Center for Real Estate and Urban Economics
DIDC	Depository Institutions Deregulation Committee
DIM	dual interest rate mortgage
DIM-GPM	dual-rate, graduated-payment loan
EAM	equity adjusted mortgage
EIR	environmental impact review
EIS	environmental impact statement
FDIC	Federal Deposit Insurance Corporation
FHA	Federal Housing Administration
FHLBB	Federal Home Loan Bank Board
FHLMC	Federal Home Loan Mortgage Corporation
FHmA	Farmers Home Administration
FNMA	Federal National Mortgage Association
FPM	fixed-payment mortgage
FRB	Federal Reserve Board
FRS	Federal Reserve System

GNMA	Government National Mortgage Association
GNPGAP	gap between potential and actual GNP
GPM	graduated-payment mortgage
HUD	Department of Housing and Urban Development
IHA	individual housing account
IRA	individual retirement account
LIC	life insurance company
MMC	money market certificate
MMDA	money market deposit account
MSB	mutual savings bank
POSSLQ	persons of opposite sex sharing the same living quarters
PSSSLQ	persons of the same sex sharing the same living quarters
SAM	shared-appreciation mortgage
SLA	savings and loan association
SSC	small savers certificate
VA	Veterans' Administration
VRM	variable-rate mortgage

*

Index

*

About the Author

Kenneth T. Rosen is a Professor of Economic Analysis and Policy and is Chairman of the Center for Real Estate and Urban Economics at the University of California at Berkeley. He specializes in real estate economics and finance and has written over 50 articles and papers and several books. He is a consultant to and on the boards of numerous private corporations and federal and state agencies dealing with housing and housing finance. He was the author of the Young Families Housing Act (1977) introduced by Senator Edward Brooke. This act introduced the GPM mortgage into the federal housing finance system. He received his Ph.D. in Economics from MIT and previously taught economics at Princeton University.